Better Homes and Gardens®

After Work
Cook Book

© Meredith Corporation, 1974. All Rights Reserved.
Printed in the United States of America. First Edition. Second Printing, 1975.
Library of Congress Catalog Card Number: 73-78909
SBN: 696-00690-1

On the cover: *After work meals become exciting when you include these dishes. Clockwise from top—* Salad Burgers, Chicken-Rice Bake, Cottage Cheese-Cucumber Salad, Cheese-Stuffed Manicotti, *or* Strawberry-Cheese Topping. *(See index for pages.)*

Above: *Let everyone assemble at the table their own Greek-Style Sandwich. Fill the hollow* Bread Envelopes *with a marinated wine-beef filling, chopped lettuce, diced tomato, diced cucumber, and sour cream dip. (See recipes, pages 21 and 22.)*

Contents

BETTER HOMES AND GARDENS BOOKS

Editorial Director: Don Dooley
Managing Editor: Malcolm E. Robinson   Art Director: John Berg
Asst. Managing Editor: Lawrence D. Clayton   Asst. Art Director: Randall Yontz
Food Editor: Nancy Morton
Senior Food Editor: Joyce Trollope
Associate Editors: Sharyl Heiken, Rosemary Corsiglia
Assistant Editors: Elizabeth Strait, Sandra Mapes
Designers: Harijs Priekulis, Tonya Rodriguez

Our seal assures you that every recipe in *After Work Cook Book* is endorsed by the Better Homes and Gardens Test Kitchen. Each recipe is tested for family appeal, practicality, and deliciousness.

To Busy Cooks Everywhere

If you're busy and you have to hurry home to cook meals for yourself, your family, or friends, *Better Homes and Gardens After Work Cook Book* is aimed squarely at you. And who isn't busy these days! Bachelors, college students, working mothers, and women employed outside the home surely are.

To help you make the best use of your limited meal preparation time, *After Work Cook Book* has been divided into three recipe sections, each based on the amount of time you can spend in the kitchen, plus a Special Helps section near the end of the book. This includes a list of basic kitchen equipment and supplies, advice on meal planning, lunch box lunches, and nutrition, plus menus using recipes from this book.

The first of the recipe sections, Cook Ahead, will be helpful when you know ahead of time that your schedule will be hectic. Here, you'll find recipes that can be made on weekends or the evening before, then put in the freezer or refrigerator until shortly before mealtime. When you are caught completely off-guard and need to prepare something in a hurry, make your selection from the In A Jiffy section. These recipes are ready to eat in 30 minutes or less. But no one is busy every night. So when you have a leisurely evening, prepare one of the recipes from the Make It Easy section. These recipes are simple to prepare and require little watching, allowing you time to relax.

Other notable features of the book include tip boxes, symbols accompanying recipes especially suitable for entertaining, and several recipes for two.

Remember, busy schedules and home-cooked meals can be coordinated. Just use the variety of recipes and helps in the *After Work Cook Book* and make the most of your limited time.

Serve tasty Barbecue-Sauced Kabobs *on a bed of parslied rice. Broil the beef, potato, and zucchini kabobs in a countertop broiler or under a regular broiler. Either way, this delicious main dish for four is ready in a jiffy. Pass the remaining zippy catsup sauce with the kabobs. (See recipe, page 41.)*

Cook Ahead

Does fitting food preparation into your after work hours mean skimpy meals night after night? If so, you'll welcome the variety of make-ahead main dishes, side dishes, and desserts in this section. Just prepare the food in your spare time on weekends or the evening before the meal, then store it in the freezer or refrigerator. When you arrive home from work, simply add the finishing touches and put the dish on to cook.

Do you like to entertain but can never find the time? Cook ahead and you won't need to get home much before the guests arrive. Plan your company menus around the recipes marked with the special entertaining symbol.

Also watch for the tip boxes scattered throughout this section. Use these ideas and hints to make meal preparation easier.

Enhance the platter of Dill-Sauced Salmon with fresh dill and lemon and lime slices. Add this make-ahead dish to your next entertaining menu. (See recipe, page 8.)

Main Dishes

Dill-Sauced Salmon

Elegant chilled salmon shown on pages 6 and 7—

- 4 fresh or frozen salmon steaks
  Boiling water
- 1 small onion, quartered
- 1 cup dairy sour cream
- 2 tablespoons finely
  chopped onion
- 2 teaspoons lemon juice
- 1 teaspoon dried dillweed

ENTERTAINING • SPECIAL •

Advance preparation: Thaw frozen fish. Place on greased rack in 10-inch skillet. Add boiling water to cover. Add quartered onion and 2 teaspoons salt. Simmer, covered, till fish flakes easily, 5 to 10 minutes. Carefully remove fish. Cover; chill well. Combine remaining ingredients; chill well.
Before serving: Spoon sour cream mixture over chilled salmon. Garnish with lemon and lime slices and fresh dillweed, if desired. Makes 4 servings.

Cauliflower-Tuna Ahoy

Advance preparation: Cook two 10-ounce packages frozen cauliflower according to package directions; drain and coarsely chop. Set aside. In large covered saucepan cook 1 cup fresh or frozen chopped onion in 2 tablespoons water. Stir in two 11-ounce cans condensed Cheddar cheese soup; one 6-ounce can sliced mushrooms, drained; ½ cup milk; 2 tablespoons snipped parsley; 1 teaspoon Worcestershire sauce; dash cayenne; and dash pepper. Drain two 6½- or 7-ounce cans tuna; break into chunks. Fold tuna and cauliflower into soup mixture. Spoon into two 1½-quart casseroles. Cover tightly. Seal; label; freeze up to 2 months.
Before serving: Bake frozen casserole, covered, at 400° for 1 hour. Uncover; continue baking till heated through, 15 to 20 minutes more. Sprinkle with paprika. Makes 2 casseroles, 4 servings each.

Tuna-Cheese Bake

Three kinds of cheese add flavor—

- 16 ounces lasagne noodles
- 1 cup fresh or frozen chopped onion
- 2 cloves garlic, minced
- ¼ cup butter or margarine
- 4 6½- or 7-ounce cans tuna, drained
  and flaked
- 2 10½-ounce cans condensed cream
  of celery soup
- ⅔ cup milk
- 1 teaspoon dried oregano, crushed
- ¼ teaspoon pepper
- 8 slices mozzarella cheese
  (12 ounces)
- 16 slices process American cheese
  (16 ounces)
- 1 cup grated Parmesan cheese

Advance preparation: In large saucepan cook lasagne noodles in boiling salted water according to package directions; drain and set aside. In medium saucepan cook onion and garlic in butter or margarine till onion is tender. Stir in tuna, cream of celery soup, milk, crushed oregano, and pepper. *In each of two 12x7x1½-inch baking dishes, layer one-fourth of the cooked lasagne noodles, half of the tuna mixture, half the mozzarella slices, half the American cheese slices, and half the grated Parmesan cheese.* Top casseroles with remaining lasagne noodles. Cover the casseroles tightly. Seal, label, and freeze up to 2 months.
Before serving: Bake the frozen tuna-cheese casserole, covered, at 400° till it is heated through, about 1½ hours. Makes 2 casseroles, 6 to 8 servings each.

Two for the time of one

Freeze this easy Cauliflower-Tuna Ahoy in a pair → of casseroles. You'll have main dishes ready to launch two meals in the time it took to prepare one.

Read Recipe Before Beginning

Before starting meal preparation, read all recipes through completely, and assemble the utensils and ingredients needed. Also, turn on the oven or broiler to preheat, if necessary. Then, food preparation will not stop while you hunt for a necessary item, but will move smoothly.

Shrimp-Noodle Bake

Keep canned shrimp and cream of shrimp soup on hand for this casserole —

> 2 cups medium noodles (about 4 ounces)
> ¼ cup fresh or frozen chopped green pepper
> 2 tablespoons butter or margarine
> 1 10½-ounce can condensed cream of shrimp soup
> ⅓ cup milk
> 1 cup shredded sharp process American cheese (4 ounces)
> 2 4½-ounce cans shrimp, drained (1¾ cups)
>
> • • •
>
> ¾ cup soft bread crumbs (1 slice)
> 1 tablespoon butter or margarine, melted

Advance preparation: Cook noodles in boiling salted water till tender but still firm, about 7 minutes. Drain noodles well. Meanwhile, in large saucepan cook chopped green pepper in 2 tablespoons butter or margarine till tender. Stir in cream of shrimp soup and milk; heat, stirring constantly, till bubbly. Add shredded cheese; stir till melted. Stir in drained shrimp and drained noodles. Turn into 1½-quart casserole. Cover; refrigerate up to 24 hours. Toss together soft bread crumbs and 1 tablespoon melted butter or margarine. Wrap and chill.
Before serving: Bake shrimp casserole, covered, at 375° for 30 minutes. Sprinkle crumb mixture atop casserole. Bake, uncovered, till heated through, about 15 minutes longer. Makes 4 or 5 servings.

Ham Croquettes

> 3 tablespoons butter or margarine
> 3 tablespoons all-purpose flour
> ¾ cup milk
> 2 cups ground fully cooked ham (about 10 ounces)
> 1 teaspoon instant minced onion
> ½ teaspoon dry mustard
> ¾ cup fine dry bread crumbs
> 1 beaten egg
> Fat for frying
> 1 8-ounce package frozen peas in cream sauce

Advance preparation: In saucepan melt butter; blend in flour. Add milk; cook and stir till thickened and bubbly. Remove from heat; stir in ham, onion, and dry mustard. Cover; refrigerate up to 24 hours.
Before serving: Shape ham mixture into 8 to 10 balls. Roll in crumbs. Shape into cones, handling lightly. Combine egg and 2 tablespoons water. Dip ham cones into egg mixture. Roll in crumbs again. Fry in deep hot fat (375°) till heated through, about 2 minutes. Drain. Meanwhile, cook peas according to package directions. Serve over croquettes. Makes 4 or 5 servings.

Apricot-Sauced Pork Chops

> ¾ cup orange juice
> ½ cup snipped dried apricots
> ¼ cup sugar
> ¼ teaspoon ground cloves
> 6 pork chops, cut ¾ inch thick

Advance preparation: In small saucepan combine juice, apricots, sugar, cloves, and ¼ cup water. Bring to boiling; cover and simmer till apricots are tender, 20 to 25 minutes. Meanwhile, trim fat from pork chops. Heat trimmings till 1 tablespoon fat accumulates; discard trimmings. Brown the chops in hot fat. Sprinkle generously with salt and pepper. Place chops in 11x7½x1½-inch baking pan. Spoon apricot mixture over. Cover; refrigerate up to 24 hours.
Before serving: Bake, covered, at 350° till tender, 45 to 50 minutes. Makes 6 servings.

Pork and Apples with Stuffing

12 pork tenderloin slices (about 4 pounds)
2 20-ounce cans pie-sliced apples, drained
½ cup packed brown sugar
2 teaspoons instant beef bouillon granules
2 cups boiling water
6 cups herb-seasoned stuffing mix
½ cup chopped celery
¼ cup butter or margarine, melted
3 tablespoons instant minced onion
1 teaspoon salt
½ teaspoon ground sage

Advance preparation: Pound tenderloin slices; trim off fat. In large skillet cook trimmings till 2 tablespoons drippings accumulate; discard trimmings. In skillet brown the meat well on both sides. Sprinkle meat with a little salt and pepper. Divide meat between two 12x7½x2-inch baking dishes. Combine apples and brown sugar. Spoon over meat. Dissolve bouillon granules in boiling water. Combine stuffing mix, celery, melted butter, instant onion, salt, and sage; toss with bouillon till moistened. Press stuffing mixture into ½-cup measure; unmold one atop each pork slice. Cover tightly. Seal; label; freeze up to 2 months.
Before serving: Bake frozen casserole, covered, at 400° till pork is done, about 1¼ hours. Makes 2 casseroles, 6 servings each.

Mincemeat Spareribs

Advance preparation: Cut 3 pounds pork spareribs in serving-size pieces. Place ribs in Dutch oven; cover with salted water. Cover pan. Bring to boiling; simmer ribs till almost tender, about 1 hour. Drain; place in shallow baking dish. Combine 1½ cups prepared mincemeat, one 10½-ounce can condensed beef broth, and 2 tablespoons vinegar. Spoon mixture over ribs. Cover; refrigerate up to 24 hours.
Before serving: Bake ribs, uncovered, at 350° for 45 to 55 minutes, spooning sauce over ribs frequently. Makes 4 servings.

Ham and Broccoli Bake

2 10½-ounce cans condensed cream of chicken soup
1 8-ounce jar process cheese spread
½ cup milk
½ cup fresh or frozen chopped onion
¼ cup butter or margarine
2 10-ounce packages frozen chopped broccoli
4 cups diced fully cooked ham
2 cups uncooked packaged precooked rice
½ teaspoon Worcestershire sauce

Advance preparation: Combine soup, cheese spread, and milk. Cook onion in butter till tender. Cook broccoli according to package directions till *almost* tender; drain. Add onion, broccoli, ham, rice, and Worcestershire to soup mixture. Turn into two 1½-quart casseroles. Cover tightly. Seal, label, and freeze up to 2 months.
Before serving: Bake, covered, at 400° for 1½ hours. Uncover; bake 30 minutes more. Makes 2 casseroles, 4 or 5 servings each.

Marinated Beef Tenderloin

½ cup catsup
1 envelope Italian salad dressing mix
1 teaspoon prepared mustard
¼ teaspoon Worcestershire sauce
1 2-pound beef tenderloin

ENTERTAINING SPECIAL

Advance preparation: Combine catsup, dressing mix, mustard, Worcestershire sauce, and ½ cup water. Pierce meat with fork on all sides. Place meat in plastic bag; set in deep bowl. Add marinade to bag; close. Refrigerate 24 hours. Occasionally press bag against meat to distribute marinade.
Before serving: Remove meat from bag, reserving marinade. Roast meat on rack in shallow roasting pan at 425° till desired doneness. Allow about 50 minutes for rare (140°) and about 60 minutes for medium (160°). Baste occasionally with reserved marinade. Heat remaining marinade. Spoon marinade over sliced meat. Serves 6 to 8.

Spaghetti and Meat Rolls

  1 beaten egg
  ¼ cup fresh or frozen chopped onion
  2 tablespoons soft bread crumbs
  ¼ teaspoon salt
  ⅛ teaspoon pepper
  1 pound ground beef
  1 8-ounce can tomato sauce
  1 cup water
  1 8-ounce package Italian dinner
      mix with spaghetti
  2 tablespoons fresh or frozen
      chopped onion
  2 tablespoons chopped celery
  1 tablespoon packed brown sugar
  1 tablespoon vinegar

Advance preparation: In bowl combine egg, ¼ cup onion, soft bread crumbs, salt, and pepper. Add ground beef; mix well. Shape into 2 rolls about 6 inches long. Place in 10x6x2-inch baking dish. Combine tomato sauce, water, sauce mix from Italian dinner, 2 tablespoons onion, celery, brown sugar, and vinegar; pour over meat rolls. Cover; refrigerate up to 24 hours.
Before serving: Bake, uncovered, at 350° for 1¼ hours, spooning sauce over meat occasionally. Just before serving, cook spaghetti from dinner mix according to package directions; drain. Turn spaghetti onto serving platter; arrange meat atop and pass sauce. Makes 4 servings.

Basic Ground Beef Mixture

Use this frozen mixture as the base for any of the following four dishes—

  2 pounds ground beef
  1 cup chopped celery
  1 cup fresh or frozen chopped onion
  ½ cup fresh or frozen chopped green
      pepper

Advance preparation: Cook all ingredients till meat is browned and vegetables are tender. Drain off excess fat. Cool quickly. Divide into three 2-cup portions in moisture-vaporproof containers. Seal, label, and freeze up to 4 months. Makes 6 cups.

Mexican Beef Bake

Tortilla pieces add crunch—

  1 16-ounce can tomatoes
  1 10-ounce can enchilada sauce
  ¼ cup sliced pitted ripe olives
  1 teaspoon salt
      Dash pepper
  2 cups frozen Basic Ground Beef
      Mixture
  ½ cup cooking oil
  8 canned or frozen tortillas
  1 cup shredded process American
      cheese (4 ounces)
  1 cup cream-style cottage cheese
  1 slightly beaten egg

In medium saucepan combine tomatoes, enchilada sauce, ripe olives, salt, and pepper. Add frozen Basic Ground Beef Mixture; simmer, covered, for 20 minutes, stirring occasionally. Heat oil in skillet. Cut *2 tortillas* into quarters. Cook the tortilla quarters and remaining whole tortillas in hot oil till crisp and brown; drain well. Set aside quartered tortillas; break up remaining tortillas. Combine American cheese, cottage cheese, and egg.

Spread *one-third* of the meat mixture in 12x7½x2-inch baking dish. Top with *half* the cheese mixture and *half* the broken tortillas. Repeat layers, ending with meat mixture. Top with quartered tortillas. Bake at 350° for 30 minutes. If desired, sprinkle an additional ½ cup shredded process American cheese over top and return to oven till cheese melts, about 5 minutes more. Let stand 5 minutes before serving. Makes 4 or 5 servings.

Cooling Tip

Do not let foods that need refrigerating stand at room temperature to cool. Since large volumes of hot food can raise the temperature inside the refrigerator or freezer, cool food quickly by placing it in a shallow container and setting this in a pan of ice water.

Slip the refrigerated Spaghetti and Meat Rolls *into the oven as soon as you come in the door. You'll have an hour to read the newspaper before cooking the spaghetti and assembling a big tossed green salad.*

Hamburger-Corn Casserole

> 2 cups frozen Basic Ground Beef
>   Mixture
> 1 10¾-ounce can condensed vegetable
>   soup
> 1 10½-ounce can condensed beef broth
> 1 17-ounce can cream-style corn
> ½ of a 7-ounce package macaroni
>   (1 cup)
> 2 cups soft bread crumbs (about
>   2½ slices bread)
> 2 tablespoons butter or margarine,
>   melted

In saucepan combine frozen beef mixture, soup, and broth. Simmer, covered, for 20 minutes, stirring occasionally. Add corn and uncooked macaroni. Turn into 2-quart casserole. Cover and bake at 375° for 50 minutes. Toss together crumbs and melted butter; sprinkle atop casserole. Bake, uncovered, 10 minutes more. Serves 4 to 6.

Oriental Skillet

> 2 cups frozen Basic Ground Beef
>   Mixture
> 1 16-ounce can chop suey vegetables,
>   drained
> 1 10-ounce package frozen peas
> • • •
> 2 tablespoons cornstarch
> 1 teaspoon sugar
> ¼ teaspoon ground ginger
> 3 tablespoons soy sauce
>   Chow mein noodles

In large saucepan or skillet combine frozen beef mixture, chop suey vegetables, frozen peas, and 1 cup water. Simmer, covered, for 20 minutes, stirring occasionally. Blend together cornstarch, sugar, and ginger; gradually stir in soy sauce and 2 tablespoons water. Add to beef mixture; cook and stir till thickened and bubbly. Serve over chow mein noodles. Serves 4.

Quick Beef Chowder

1 16-ounce can tomatoes, cut up
1 10½-ounce can condensed cream of
  celery soup
1 8-ounce can whole kernel corn
2 tablespoons snipped parsley
2 cups frozen Basic Ground Beef
  Mixture (see recipe, page 12)

In large saucepan stir tomatoes into celery soup; stir in undrained corn, parsley, and ¼ teaspoon salt. Add frozen beef mixture. Simmer, covered, for 20 minutes, stirring occasionally. Makes 4 or 5 servings.

Potato-Topped Stew

2 tablespoons all-purpose flour
1 pound beef stew meat, cut in
  ¾-inch cubes
2 tablespoons shortening
1 10½-ounce can condensed golden
  mushroom soup
1 tablespoon instant minced onion
¼ teaspoon dried basil, crushed
1 10-ounce package frozen mixed
  vegetables
⅓ cup dry red wine
  Packaged instant mashed potatoes
  (enough for 4 servings)
½ cup shredded process American
  cheese (2 ounces)

Advance preparation: Combine flour, 1 teaspoon salt, and dash pepper in plastic or paper bag. Shake meat cubes with flour mixture to coat. In Dutch oven brown the meat in hot shortening. Stir in soup, instant minced onion, basil, and ¾ cup water. Cover; cook, stirring occasionally, for 30 minutes. Add mixed vegetables; continue cooking till meat is tender, about 30 minutes more. Stir in wine. Spoon into 1½-quart casserole. Cover tightly. Seal, label, and freeze up to 2 months.
Before serving: Bake frozen casserole, covered, at 400° for 1¼ hours. Prepare potatoes, following package directions. Spoon around edge; sprinkle with cheese. Bake, uncovered, 15 minutes longer. Serves 4.

Herbed Round Steak

Advance preparation: Using one 2-pound beef round steak cut ¾ inch thick, divide steak into 6 portions. Trim fat. Season meat with ½ teaspoon salt and ⅛ teaspoon pepper. In skillet brown the meat in 2 tablespoons cooking oil; remove meat. In same skillet cook 1 medium onion, sliced, till tender. Return meat to skillet; add ½ cup water. Simmer, covered, for 1 hour. Turn into 12x7½x2-inch baking dish; reserve drippings. Combine one 10½-ounce can condensed cream of celery soup and ¾ cup milk; stir into reserved drippings. Stir in ½ teaspoon dried oregano, crushed, and ¼ teaspoon dried thyme, crushed. Pour over meat. Cover; refrigerate up to 24 hours.
Before serving: Bake, covered, at 350° till heated through, about 1 hour. Serves 6.

Easy Moussaka

Advance preparation: Combine 1 medium eggplant, chopped, and ¼ cup water. Cover; simmer till tender. Turn into 2-quart casserole. In skillet cook 1½ pounds ground beef, ½ cup fresh or frozen chopped onion, and 1 small clove garlic, minced, till beef is browned; drain. Stir in 2 cups finely shredded cabbage, one 8-ounce can tomato sauce, 1 tablespoon Worcestershire sauce, 1 teaspoon salt, ¼ teaspoon pepper, and dash ground nutmeg. Cover; cook 10 minutes. Stir in 1 cup shredded sharp process American cheese. Spoon over eggplant. Cover; refrigerate up to 24 hours.
Before serving: Bake, covered, at 350° for 45 minutes. Uncover; top with ½ cup shredded sharp process American cheese. Bake 15 minutes more. Makes 6 servings.

Make-Ahead Tip

Most casseroles can be refrigerated for as long as 24 hours before baking. Just remember to cover tightly before chilling and allow some extra baking time.

Ravioli Florentine

    2 pounds ground beef
    1 15-ounce can pizza sauce
    2 15-ounce cans spinach
    3 cups cream-style cottage cheese
        with chives
    2 15-ounce cans ravioli in tomato
        sauce
    ⅓ cup grated Parmesan cheese

Advance preparation: Brown the beef; drain. Stir in pizza sauce. Drain spinach. In *each* of two 10x6x2-inch baking dishes layer *half* spinach, *one-fourth* meat mixture, *half* cottage cheese, and *half* ravioli. Top with remaining meat mixture. Cover tightly. Seal, label, and freeze up to 2 months.
Before serving: Bake frozen casserole, covered, at 400° for 1¼ hours. Uncover; bake till heated through, about 30 minutes. Sprinkle *each casserole* with about 3 tablespoons Parmesan. Let stand 10 minutes. Makes 2 casseroles, 4 servings each.

Make-Ahead Oriental Beef Stew

    1½ pounds beef stew meat, cut in
            1-inch cubes
      2 tablespoons cooking oil
      ½ cup fresh or frozen chopped onion
      1 small clove garlic, minced
      1 16-ounce can tomatoes
      ¼ cup soy sauce
      ½ teaspoon ground ginger
      1 large green pepper
      2 tablespoons cornstarch

Advance preparation: Brown the beef in hot oil. Add onion, garlic, and 1 cup water. Simmer, covered, for 1¼ hours. Cover; chill. Skim off fat. Spoon meat into freezer container. Seal, label, and freeze.
Before serving: Cut up tomatoes; in saucepan combine with frozen beef, soy, and ginger. Cover. Cook over low heat till thawed and boiling, 20 to 30 minutes; stir often. Cut pepper in strips; add to stew. Simmer, covered, for 5 minutes. Stir in mixture of cornstarch and 2 tablespoons cold water. Cook and stir till bubbly. Serves 4.

Sour Cream Meatballs

    1 cup crushed corn chips
    1 cup milk
    1 clove garlic, minced
    3 tablespoons snipped parsley
    2 pounds ground beef
    3 tablespoons butter or margarine
    1 cup fresh or frozen chopped onion
    2 tablespoons all-purpose flour
    1 10½-ounce can condensed beef broth
    1 teaspoon Worcestershire sauce
    1 cup dairy sour cream

Advance preparation: Mix first 4 ingredients, 1 teaspoon salt, and ⅛ teaspoon pepper. Mix in beef. Shape into sixty 1-inch balls. Bake in large, shallow baking pan at 375° for 20 minutes; shake pan often to turn meatballs. Cover; chill. In 3-quart saucepan melt butter. Add onion; cook till tender. Blend in flour. Add broth, Worcestershire, and ½ cup water. Cook and stir till bubbly. Cover; refrigerate up to 24 hours.
Before serving: Heat sauce. Add meatballs; heat through. Stir in sour cream. Heat through (*do not boil*). Serves 6 to 8.

Steak Parisienne

    1 beef T-bone steak (about 1½ pounds)
    ¼ pound fresh mushrooms
    5 tablespoons olive oil
    ½ cup dry red wine
    ¼ cup red wine vinegar
    ½ teaspoon lemon pepper seasoning
    ¼ teaspoon dried thyme, crushed
    ¼ teaspoon dried basil, crushed
    ¼ teaspoon dried marjoram, crushed
    6 cherry tomatoes
    6 canned artichoke hearts

· ENTERTAINING · SPECIAL

Advance preparation: Broil steak till rare. Chill. Cut into ½-inch slices. Slice mushrooms; cook in *2 tablespoons* oil till just tender. Mix remaining oil, wine, vinegar, seasonings, and 1 teaspoon salt. Pour over meat and mushrooms. Chill 3 hours.
Before serving: Drain meat. Arrange meat, mushrooms, tomatoes, and artichokes on platter. Spoon dressing over. Serves 2 or 3.

Do-Ahead Beef Noodle Bake

    4 ounces noodles
    1 pound ground beef
    ½ cup fresh or frozen chopped onion
    ¼ cup fresh or frozen chopped green
        pepper
    1 15-ounce can tomato sauce
    ½ teaspoon seasoned salt
    2 cups cream-style cottage cheese
    1 3-ounce package cream cheese,
        softened

Advance preparation: Cook noodles in boiling, salted water till tender. Brown beef, onion, and green pepper; drain off fat. Stir in tomato sauce, seasoned salt, and ¼ teaspoon pepper. Blend cheeses till fluffy. In buttered 10x6x2-inch baking dish layer noodles, cheese mixture, and meat sauce. Cover; refrigerate up to 24 hours.
Before serving: Bake at 350° till heated through, about 40 minutes. Serves 6.

Cheesy Chicken Rolls

    4 whole large chicken breasts,
        skinned, boned, and halved
        lengthwise
    2 ounces process Swiss cheese, cut
        in 8 strips
    2 tablespoons crumbled blue cheese
    1 cup fine dry bread crumbs
    1 tablespoon butter, melted
        All-purpose flour
    2 beaten eggs

Advance preparation: Place chicken pieces, boned side up, between clear plastic wrap. Pound from center out to form cutlets ¼ inch thick. Peel off wrap; sprinkle with salt. Place a strip of Swiss cheese at end of each cutlet; sprinkle with blue cheese. Beginning with short side, roll up jelly-roll fashion, tucking in sides. Press end to seal well. Mix crumbs and butter. Coat each roll with flour; dip in eggs. Roll in crumbs. Place in shallow baking pan. Cover. Refrigerate till well chilled, 1 to 24 hours.
Before serving: Bake, uncovered, at 350° till done, about 45 minutes. Serves 4 to 6.

Chicken Roll-Ups

    4 whole medium chicken breasts,
        skinned and boned
    2 tablespoons butter, softened
    2 tablespoons snipped parsley
    ⅛ teaspoon dried marjoram, crushed
        All-purpose flour
        Milk
    1 2⅜-ounce package seasoned coating
        mix for chicken

Advance preparation: Place chicken breasts, boned side up, between clear plastic wrap. Pound from center out till about ¼ inch thick. Peel off wrap; season with salt. Mix butter, parsley, and marjoram; spread on one side of chicken pieces, spreading not quite to edge. Roll up jelly-roll fashion, tucking in sides. Press seams to seal well. Coat each chicken roll with flour. Dip in milk, then roll in coating mix. Cover lightly; refrigerate up to 24 hours.
Before serving: Bake in shallow baking pan at 400° about 35 minutes. Serves 4.

Individual Chicken Casseroles

    ½ cup fresh or frozen chopped onion
    6 tablespoons butter or margarine
    ½ cup all-purpose flour
    3 cups chicken broth
    3 cups cubed cooked chicken
    1 10-ounce package frozen peas and
        carrots, cooked and drained
    ¼ cup chopped canned pimiento

Advance preparation: Cook onion in butter till tender. Blend in flour and 1 teaspoon salt. Stir in chicken broth. Cook and stir till thickened and bubbly. Stir in chicken, peas and carrots, and pimiento. Line 6 to 8 individual casseroles with heavy foil, leaving enough overlapping to seal. Spoon in chicken mixture; seal foil. Freeze. When solid, remove foil packets from casseroles. Label; freeze up to 2 months.
Before serving: Remove foil; set food blocks into casseroles. Bake, covered, at 400° about 1 hour, stirring once or twice toward end of baking time. Serves 6 to 8.

Lazy Paella

  1 3-pound ready-to-cook broiler-
      fryer chicken, cut up
  2 tablespoons cooking oil
1½ cups chicken broth
  8 ounces shelled shrimp
  1 8½-ounce can peas, drained
  1 6-ounce package saffron rice mix
  1 3-ounce can sliced mushrooms,
      drained
  ½ envelope onion soup mix (¼ cup)

Advance preparation: Brown chicken in oil. Season with salt and pepper. Mix remaining ingredients; spread in 3-quart casserole. Top with chicken. Sprinkle with paprika, if desired. Cover; chill up to 24 hours.
Before serving: Bake, covered, at 350° about 1¼ hours. Makes 4 servings.

Orange Chicken

½ cup cooking oil
½ teaspoon grated orange peel
½ cup orange juice
 1 teaspoon instant minced onion
½ teaspoon Worcestershire sauce
 1 2½- to 3-pound ready-to-cook
    broiler-fryer chicken, cut up

Advance preparation: Mix first 5 ingredients and ½ teaspoon salt. Place chicken in plastic bag. Pour oil mixture over. Close bag; place in bowl. Refrigerate 24 hours; press occasionally to distribute marinade.
Before serving: Drain chicken; reserve marinade. Place chicken, skin side down, in broiler pan (no rack). Broil 4 to 5 inches from heat about 40 minutes. Brush often with marinade; turn once. Serves 3 or 4.

Lazy Paella makes a striking entrée for a small company dinner. The chicken-shrimp casserole mixes saffron rice with mushrooms and peas for a brightly decorated main dish. Paprika adds a colorful garnish.

Chicken-Vegetable Strata

Advance preparation: Cook one 8-ounce package frozen mixed vegetables with onion sauce according to package directions. Stir in 1 cup shredded sharp process American cheese, ¾ cup milk, and ½ teaspoon poultry seasoning; cool slightly. Stir in 2 beaten eggs. Cut 3 slices bread in 1-inch cubes. Place *half* bread in 10x6x2-inch baking dish. Top with 1½ cups cubed cooked chicken, then remaining bread. Pour vegetable mixture over. Cover; refrigerate up to 24 hours. Toss 1 cup soft bread crumbs with 2 tablespoons butter, melted. Wrap; chill.
Before serving: Sprinkle crumbs atop casserole. Bake, uncovered, at 325° till set, 50 to 60 minutes. Let stand 10 minutes before serving. Makes 4 to 6 servings.

Chicken and Rice Balls

  ½ cup chopped celery
  ¼ cup sliced green onion
  2 tablespoons butter or margarine
  2 tablespoons all-purpose flour
  ¼ cup chicken broth
  2 cups cooked short grain rice
1½ cups diced cooked chicken
  ½ cup shredded process
      American cheese (2 ounces)
  1 beaten egg
  ½ teaspoon poultry seasoning
  ½ cup cornflake crumbs
  1 10¾-ounce can condensed cream
      of mushroom soup
  ⅓ cup milk
  2 tablespoons sliced green onion

Advance preparation: Cook celery and ¼ cup onion in butter till tender. Blend in flour; add broth. Cook and stir till thick. Stir in next 5 ingredients and ½ teaspoon salt. Shape mixture into 12 balls; roll in crumbs. Place in 13x9x2-inch baking pan. Cover; refrigerate up to 24 hours.
Before serving: Bake, uncovered, at 350° for 35 to 40 minutes. Meanwhile, for sauce combine soup, milk, and 2 tablespoons onion; heat through. Serve sauce over chicken balls. Makes 4 servings.

Chicken-Noodle Dinner

  2 envelopes chicken-noodle soup mix
  1 6-ounce can sliced mushrooms
  2 6-ounce cans evaporated milk
  ½ cup butter or margarine
  ½ cup all-purpose flour
  1 10-ounce package frozen mixed
      vegetables
  4 cups diced cooked chicken
  4 eggs

Advance preparation: In saucepan combine soup mix and 3 cups water; bring to boiling. Reduce heat; cover and simmer 5 minutes. Strain, reserving broth. Divide noodles in half; freeze in two packages. Drain mushrooms, reserving liquid. Combine reserved broth, mushroom liquid, and evaporated milk. In saucepan melt butter or margarine; blend in flour, ½ teaspoon salt, and ¼ teaspoon pepper. Add broth mixture; cook and stir till thickened. Break up frozen vegetables with fork; add to broth mixture along with mushrooms and chicken. Turn into two 1½-quart casseroles. Cover tightly. Seal, label, and freeze up to 2 months.
Before serving: Bake frozen casserole, covered, at 400° for 1¼ hours; stir once or twice. *For each casserole,* beat 2 eggs; combine eggs, one package of the frozen noodles, and ¼ teaspoon salt. Spoon atop casserole. Bake, covered, 10 minutes more. Makes 2 casseroles, 6 to 8 servings each.

Stuffed Baked Franks

Advance preparation: Slit 5 or 6 large frankfurters (1 pound) lengthwise almost to opposite side. Cook ¼ cup minced onion in 1 tablespoon butter till tender. Mix 2 cups herb-seasoned stuffing mix, the onion, ¾ cup water, ¼ cup catsup, and 1 tablespoon sweet pickle relish. Mound stuffing into slit franks. Place on baking sheet. Cover; refrigerate up to 24 hours.
Before serving: Bake at 400° for 10 to 15 minutes. Cut 3 slices sharp process American cheese into strips. Top franks with cheese strips; bake till cheese melts, about 3 minutes. Makes 5 or 6 servings.

Frankfurter-Cheese Casserole

Advance preparation: Cook ¾ cup macaroni in boiling salted water till tender, about 8 minutes; drain well. Cook ⅓ cup fresh or frozen chopped onion and ⅓ cup fresh or frozen chopped green pepper in 2 tablespoons butter till tender. Blend in 3 tablespoons all-purpose flour and 1 teaspoon *each* Worcestershire sauce and prepared mustard. Add 1 cup milk. Cook and stir till thickened and bubbly. Stir in macaroni, 1½ cups cream-style cottage cheese, and 6 frankfurters, thinly sliced. Turn into 1½-quart casserole. Cover; refrigerate up to 24 hours. Toss 1½ cups soft bread crumbs and 2 tablespoons butter, melted. Wrap; chill.
Before serving: Bake casserole, covered, at 350° for 40 minutes, gently stirring occasionally. Sprinkle crumbs on top. Bake, uncovered, till heated through, about 10 minutes more. Let stand 5 to 10 minutes before serving. Makes 4 to 6 servings.

Western Baked Beans

Arrange Polish sausages in a pinwheel atop—

    4 slices bacon
    1 cup fresh or frozen chopped onion
    1 clove garlic, minced
    1 16-ounce can kidney beans, drained
    1 16-ounce can lima beans, drained
    1 16-ounce can butter beans, drained
    1 14-ounce jar baked beans in
        molasses sauce
    ½ cup catsup
    ½ cup dry red wine
    3 tablespoons packed brown sugar
    ½ teaspoon dry mustard
    6 Polish sausages, halved diagonally

Advance preparation: Cook bacon till crisp; remove and crumble. Cook onion and garlic in bacon drippings till onion is tender. Combine onion, garlic, beans, catsup, wine, brown sugar, dry mustard, bacon, and ¼ teaspoon pepper. Spoon into 3-quart casserole. Cover; refrigerate up to 24 hours.
Before serving: Arrange sausages atop beans. Bake, uncovered, at 375° till heated through, about 1 hour. Makes 6 servings.

Sausage Lasagne

    4 ounces lasagne noodles
    ½ pound Italian sausage
    1 8-ounce can tomatoes
    1 8-ounce can tomato sauce with
        onion
    ¼ teaspoon dried oregano, crushed
    1 beaten egg
    1½ cups fresh ricotta *or* cream-style
        cottage cheese
    ¼ cup grated Parmesan cheese
    1½ teaspoons dried parsley flakes
    1 6-ounce package sliced mozzarella
        cheese

Advance preparation: Cook noodles according to package directions; drain. Cook sausage till browned; drain off fat. Mix sausage, tomatoes, tomato sauce, and oregano. Mix egg, ricotta or cottage cheese, Parmesan, and parsley. Place *half* noodles in 10x6x2-inch baking dish. Spread with *half* cheese mixture; top with *half* mozzarella. Cover with *half* sausage mixture. Repeat layers. Cover; refrigerate up to 24 hours.
Before serving: Bake, covered, at 375° about 50 minutes. Let stand 10 minutes. Serves 6.

Tangy Lamb Shoulder Chops

    4 lamb shoulder chops, cut ¾ inch
        thick (about 2 pounds)
    1 tablespoon shortening
    ¼ cup hot-style catsup
    1 teaspoon dried basil, crushed
    4 onion slices
    4 green pepper rings
    ¼ cup shredded process American
        cheese (1 ounce)

Advance preparation: Trim excess fat from chops. Brown the chops in hot shortening. Sprinkle with ½ teaspoon salt and dash pepper. Place in 9x9x2-inch baking dish. Spread with catsup; sprinkle with basil. Top with onion and green pepper. Cover; refrigerate up to 24 hours.
Before serving: Bake, covered, at 350° about 1 hour. Uncover; sprinkle cheese inside peppers. Bake till cheese melts. Serves 4.

Serve hearty Stroganoff Steak Sandwiches with mugs of beer for a man-pleasing supper. The meat gets its unusual flavor from a beer marinade. French bread, onions, and a sour cream topper complete the sandwich.

Ham Loaf Sandwiches

2 beaten eggs
½ cup coarsely crushed saltine
   crackers (10 crackers)
½ cup milk
¼ cup packed brown sugar
2 tablespoons vinegar
1 tablespoon prepared mustard
1½ pounds fully cooked ham, ground
   (about 5 cups)
½ pound ground pork
   Sliced rye bread
   Sweet pickle relish

Advance preparation: Combine eggs, crushed crackers, milk, brown sugar, vinegar, mustard, and dash pepper; mix in ham and pork. Pat into 9x5x3-inch loaf pan. Bake at 350° about 1¼ hours. Drain off fat. Refrigerate in pan till well chilled.
Before serving: Slice loaf. Serve on rye bread with sweet pickle relish and additional mustard. Makes 6 to 8 sandwiches.

Tuna-Cabbage Buns

Pack Cheddar cheese sticks and potato chips in the lunch box with this tasty sandwich —

1 cup chopped cabbage
1 6½- or 7-ounce can tuna, drained
   and flaked
⅓ cup mayonnaise or salad dressing
2 tablespoons chopped green onion
   with tops
     • • •
   Butter or margarine, softened
4 hamburger buns, split

Advance preparation: In small mixing bowl combine chopped cabbage, flaked tuna, mayonnaise or salad dressing, and chopped green onion with tops; mix well. Cover; refrigerate up to 24 hours.
Before serving: Spread butter on bottom halves of hamburger buns. Spread with tuna mixture. Cover with top halves of hamburger buns. Garnish sandwiches with pickle slices, if desired. Makes 4 sandwiches.

Shrimpwich

A hearty sandwich for one or two —

    1 4½-ounce can small shrimp, drained
    1 hard-cooked egg, chopped
    ¼ cup mayonnaise or salad dressing
    1 tablespoon chili sauce
    ½ teaspoon instant minced onion
    1 individual French roll
      Lettuce

Advance preparation: In small bowl combine shrimp, egg, mayonnaise or salad dressing, chili sauce, and instant minced onion. Cover tightly; chill up to 24 hours.
Before serving: Cut thin slice from top of roll; hollow out. Fill roll with shrimp mixture. Add lettuce. Makes 1 sandwich.

Stroganoff Steak Sandwiches

    ⅔ cup beer
    ⅓ cup cooking oil
    1 teaspoon salt
    ¼ teaspoon garlic powder
    ¼ teaspoon pepper
    2 pounds beef flank steak, cut
        1 inch thick
    2 tablespoons butter or margarine
    ½ teaspoon paprika
    4 cups sliced onion
   12 slices French bread, toasted
    1 cup dairy sour cream
    ½ teaspoon prepared horseradish

ENTERTAINING SPECIAL

Advance preparation: Combine beer, oil, salt, garlic powder, and pepper. Pour into shallow dish. Place steak in beer mixture. Cover and marinate overnight in refrigerator.
Before serving: Drain steak; pat dry with paper toweling. Broil steak 3 inches from heat till desired doneness. (Allow 5 to 7 minutes on each side for medium-rare.) Melt butter; blend in paprika and dash salt. Add onion; cook till tender. Thinly slice meat on the diagonal across grain. *For each sandwich,* arrange meat over 2 slices bread. Top with onions. Warm sour cream; stir in horseradish and spoon over onions. Sprinkle with additional paprika, if desired. Makes 6 sandwiches.

Freezing Sandwiches

Keep frozen sandwiches on hand for lunches or simple suppers. Make several sandwiches at once and then store them in the freezer for up to 2 weeks.

    Sandwich fillings that freeze well include cream cheese, hard-cooked egg yolks, sliced or ground cooked meat and poultry, tuna, salmon, and peanut butter. *Do not freeze* sandwiches containing lettuce, celery, tomatoes, cucumbers, egg whites, jelly, or mayonnaise.

Greek-Style Sandwiches

Colorful sandwiches shown on page 2 —

    ½ cup dry red wine
    2 tablespoons olive or cooking oil
    1 small clove garlic, minced
    ½ teaspoon dried oregano, crushed
    ½ teaspoon salt
      Dash freshly ground pepper
    1 pound beef sirloin steak,
        cut ½ inch thick
    1 tablespoon butter
   4 or 5 Bread Envelopes
        (see recipe, page 22)
    2 cups chopped lettuce
    1 cup diced, seeded tomato (1 large)
    ⅔ cup diced, seeded cucumber (about
        1 small)
    1 cup sour cream dip with chives

ENTERTAINING SPECIAL

Advance preparation: Combine wine, oil, garlic, oregano, salt, and pepper. Cut steak into strips, 2 inches long and ¼ inch wide. Pour wine mixture over beef strips. Cover; refrigerate up to 24 hours.
Before serving: Drain beef strips well. In medium skillet cook *half* the meat in hot butter, stirring to brown on all sides, 2 to 3 minutes. Repeat with remaining meat strips. With sharp knife, open one side of each thawed Bread Envelope to make a pocket. Fill pocket with cooked meat strips, chopped lettuce, diced tomato, diced cucumber, and sour cream dip with chives. Makes 4 or 5 sandwiches.

Bread Envelopes

Use these for Greek-Style Sandwiches (page 21) —

> **3½ to 4 cups all-purpose flour**
> **1 package active dry yeast**
> **2 tablespoons cooking oil**
> **¼ teaspoon sugar**

Advance preparation: In large mixer bowl combine 1½ cups flour and yeast. Combine oil, sugar, 1¼ cups warm water (110°), and 1 teaspoon salt. Add to yeast mixture; beat on low speed of electric mixer for ½ minute, scraping sides constantly. Beat 3 minutes at high speed. By hand, stir in enough of the remaining flour to make moderately stiff dough. Turn out on floured surface; knead till smooth and elastic, about 5 minutes. Cover; let rise 45 minutes.

Punch down and divide in 12 equal parts. Shape into balls; cover and let rest 10 minutes. Roll each ball on lightly floured surface to 5-inch circle, beginning at center and rolling to edges. (Do not roll back and forth.) Place 2 inches apart on ungreased baking sheet. Cover; let rest 20 to 30 minutes. Bake at 400° till puffed and browned, 10 to 12 minutes. Remove from baking sheet; immediately wrap individually in foil. Cool. Label; freeze. Makes 12.

Salad Burgers

Relish-topped sandwiches shown on the cover —

> **¼ cup vinegar**
> **2 tablespoons sugar**
> **1 cup chopped onion**
> **1 large tomato, diced**
> **½ medium cucumber, thinly sliced**
> **2 pounds ground beef**
> **8 hamburger buns, split and toasted**

Advance preparation: Mix vinegar, sugar, ¼ cup water, 1 teaspoon salt, and ⅛ teaspoon pepper. Add vegetables. Cover; chill.
Before serving: Mix meat, 1½ teaspoons salt, and ⅛ teaspoon pepper; shape into 8 patties. Broil 3 inches from heat till done, about 10 minutes, turning once. Place on bottoms of buns. Drain vegetable mixture; spoon onto patties. Add bun tops. Serves 8.

Horseradish-Sauced Beefwiches

Advance preparation: In saucepan combine 2 beaten egg yolks, 2 tablespoons freshly grated horseradish, 2 tablespoons vinegar, 1 tablespoon sugar, 1 tablespoon prepared mustard, 1 tablespoon water, and ½ teaspoon salt. Mix well. Cook and stir over low heat till thickened, about 2 minutes. Remove from heat. Stir till smooth. Refrigerate till well chilled, 3 to 24 hours.
Before serving: Whip ½ cup whipping cream; fold into chilled horseradish mixture. Assemble sandwiches of buttered rye bread, lettuce, and sliced, chilled cooked roast beef. Top with dollops of horseradish mixture. Makes about 1⅓ cups sauce.

Sweet-Sour Chicken Mold

> **2 packages sour cream sauce mix**
>   **(each enough for 1 cup sauce)**
> **2 3-ounce packages lemon-flavored**
>   **gelatin**
> **2 cups boiling water**
> **½ cup cold water**
> **2 tablespoons lemon juice**
> **1 teaspoon dried dillweed**
> **1 medium green pepper, seeded and**
>   **quartered**
> **1 medium cucumber, peeled,**
>   **quartered, and seeded**
> **1 small carrot, sliced**
> **2 5-ounce cans boned chicken,**
>   **drained and cut up**
> **Assorted fresh vegetables**

ENTERTAINING • SPECIAL •

Advance preparation: Prepare sauce mix according to package directions (including letting stand 10 minutes). Dissolve gelatin in boiling water; add sour cream sauce, cold water, lemon juice, and dillweed. Beat till blended. Chill till partially set. Place green pepper, cucumber, and carrot in blender container; cover with *cold* water. Cover; blend just till coarsely chopped. Drain well; stir chopped vegetables and chicken into gelatin mixture. Turn into 7½-cup ring mold. Chill till firm.
Before serving: Unmold and fill center with fresh vegetables. Makes 8 servings.

Chicken-Raspberry Salad

Advance preparation: Sieve one 10-ounce package frozen raspberries, thawed, by pushing through strainer. Add enough water to make 1 cup liquid. In saucepan combine ⅓ cup sugar, 1 envelope unflavored gelatin, and dash salt. Stir in raspberry mixture. Heat and stir till gelatin dissolves. Stir in ½ cup cold water and 3 tablespoons lemon juice. Chill till partially set. Fold in 1 cup small cantaloupe balls. Pour into 3½-cup ring mold. Chill till firm. Combine 1½ cups cubed cooked chicken, ½ cup diced celery, ⅓ cup mayonnaise, 2 tablespoons chopped sweet pickle, and ¼ teaspoon salt. Toss lightly. Cover; chill up to 24 hours.

Before serving: Unmold gelatin and fill center with chicken mixture. Serves 4.

Ham-Rice Salad

  1 10-ounce package frozen rice pilaf
  ¼ cup mayonnaise or salad dressing
  2 teaspoons vinegar
  ½ teaspoon curry powder
  1 cup cubed fully cooked ham
  1 medium apple, chopped (1 cup)
      • • •
  Lettuce cups

Advance preparation: Cook rice pilaf according to package directions; cool. In mixing bowl stir together mayonnaise or salad dressing, vinegar, and curry powder. Add cooked rice pilaf, ham, and apple. Cover; refrigerate up to 24 hours.

Before serving: Spoon chilled salad mixture into lettuce cups. Makes 4 servings.

Sour cream sauce mix, lemon juice, and dillweed combine with lemon-flavored gelatin to produce the distinctive flavors in Sweet-Sour Chicken Mold. *To serve, fill the center with an assortment of crisp, fresh vegetables.*

Macaroni-Frank Salad

Advance preparation: Cook 2 cups macaroni in boiling, salted water till tender. Drain. Pour ½ cup Italian salad dressing over macaroni; refrigerate at least 4 hours. Stir in 2 cups diced celery; 4 or 5 frankfurters, thinly sliced; ¼ cup finely snipped parsley; and ¼ cup sweet pickle relish. Stir in ½ cup dairy sour cream. Refrigerate up to 24 hours. Makes 6 servings.

Beef Supper Salad

   ½ cup mayonnaise or salad dressing
   1 tablespoon chili sauce
   1 tablespoon sweet pickle relish
   2 cups cubed cooked beef
   1 8-ounce can kidney beans, drained
   1 cup sliced celery
   ⅓ cup chopped onion
   2 hard-cooked eggs, chopped

Advance preparation: Combine first 3 ingredients and ¼ teaspoon salt. Combine beef, beans, celery, onion, and eggs. Pour dressing over bean mixture; toss lightly. Refrigerate up to 24 hours. Serves 4 or 5.

Fruited Chicken Salad

   1 8-ounce can jellied cranberry
      sauce, chilled
   1 13¼-ounce can pineapple tidbits
   ½ cup dairy sour cream
   1 3-ounce package cream cheese,
      softened
   Dash salt
   1½ cups cubed cooked chicken
   ¾ cup sliced celery
   ½ cup chopped walnuts
   2 tablespoons chopped green pepper

Advance preparation: Cut cranberry sauce into cubes; chill. Drain pineapple. Beat together sour cream, cheese, and salt. Fold in chicken, pineapple, celery, nuts, and green pepper. Refrigerate up to 24 hours.
Before serving: Top chicken mixture with cranberry cubes. Makes 4 or 5 servings.

Chicken-Wild Rice Salad

   1 6-ounce package long grain and
      wild rice mix
   2 cups cubed cooked chicken
   ¼ cup chopped green pepper
   2 tablespoons chopped canned
      pimiento
   ½ cup mayonnaise or salad dressing
   2 tablespoons Russian salad dressing
   1 tablespoon lemon juice
   ¼ teaspoon salt
   1 or 2 avocados

Advance preparation: Cook rice mix according to package directions; cool. Combine chicken, green pepper, and pimiento. Stir in rice. Mix mayonnaise, Russian dressing, juice, and ¼ teaspoon salt; toss with rice mixture. Refrigerate up to 24 hours.
Before serving: Peel and slice avocados. Spoon salad over slices. Serves 4 to 6.

Shrimp-Tomato Vinaigrette

   4 tomatoes
   1 pound fresh or frozen shelled
      shrimp, cooked (2 cups)
   1 6-ounce package frozen pea pods,
      thawed and drained
   2 tablespoons sliced green onion
      with tops
   ½ cup salad oil
   ¼ cup dry white wine
   ¼ cup wine vinegar
   1 envelope Italian salad dressing
      mix
   1 to 2 tablespoons capers, well
      drained

Advance preparation: With stem ends down cut tomatoes into wedges, *cutting to, but not through base.* Spread wedges apart slightly; salt lightly. Cover; chill. Combine shrimp, pea pods, and onion. Mix remaining ingredients and dash pepper; pour over shrimp mixture. Cover; chill several hours.
Before serving: Drain shrimp mixture, reserving marinade. Spoon mixture into tomato shells on serving plate. Pass remaining marinade, if desired. Serves 4.

Chef's Rice Salad

Advance preparation: Bring 1½ cups water and ½ teaspoon salt to boiling. Add one 10-ounce package frozen peas. Return to boil; cook 2 minutes. Stir in 1 cup uncooked packaged precooked rice; cover. Remove from heat; let stand 5 minutes. Stir in ¾ cup mayonnaise, ¼ cup chopped dill pickle, 1 teaspoon grated onion, and dash pepper. Refrigerate up to 24 hours.
Before serving: Spoon rice mixture onto lettuce-lined plates. Top with *half* of a 12-ounce can chopped ham, cut in thin strips, and ½ cup Swiss cheese cut in thin strips (2 ounces). Makes 4 or 5 servings.

Cranberry-Tuna Salad Mold

    1 3-ounce package lemon-flavored
        gelatin
    ½ cup orange juice
    1 16-ounce can jellied cranberry
        sauce
    2 or 3 drops red food coloring
    1 6½- or 7-ounce can tuna, drained
        and flaked
    ½ cup chopped celery
    1 hard-cooked egg, chopped
    ¼ cup sliced pimiento-stuffed green
        olives
    1 tablespoon finely chopped onion
    1 cup mayonnaise or salad dressing
    ½ teaspoon salt
        Dash pepper
    1 envelope unflavored gelatin

Advance preparation: In saucepan combine lemon-flavored gelatin, orange juice, and ½ cup water; cook and stir till boiling and gelatin dissolves. Beat jellied cranberry sauce and red food coloring till smooth; stir into gelatin mixture. Turn into 6½-cup mold. Chill till almost firm.

Combine tuna, celery, egg, olives, and onion. Fold in mayonnaise, salt, and dash pepper. Soften unflavored gelatin in ½ cup cold water; heat and stir till dissolved. Stir into tuna mixture. Chill till partially set; spoon over cranberry layer. Chill till firm. Makes 5 or 6 servings.

Weary appetites perk up at the sight of Shrimp-Tomato Vinaigrette. This marinated main dish salad will become a favorite for hot-weather meals.

Macaroni-Shrimp Salad

    ¾ cup small macaroni shells
    8 ounces fresh or frozen shelled
        shrimp, cooked and cut in half
        lengthwise
    ⅓ cup chopped celery
    2 tablespoons sliced pimiento-
        stuffed green olives
    1 tablespoon snipped parsley
    ½ cup mayonnaise or salad dressing
    2 tablespoons red wine vinegar
    2 teaspoons lemon juice
    ¼ teaspoon garlic salt
    ¼ teaspoon dry mustard
    ¼ teaspoon paprika

Advance preparation: Cook macaroni in boiling salted water till tender; drain. Combine macaroni, shrimp, celery, olives, and parsley. Blend together mayonnaise, wine vinegar, lemon juice, garlic salt, mustard, and paprika; toss with shrimp mixture. Refrigerate up to 24 hours. Serves 4.

Side Dishes and Desserts

Horseradish Bloody Mary

A perfect meal-starter—

Advance preparation: In large pitcher combine one 46-ounce can tomato juice, 2 cups vodka, 2 tablespoons lemon juice, 1 tablespoon prepared horseradish, 1 teaspoon Worcestershire sauce, ¾ teaspoon salt, and few drops bottled hot pepper sauce. Refrigerate several hours or overnight.
Before serving: Pour mixture over ice. Use celery stick stirrers. Makes 2 quarts.

Cream of Avocado Soup

    2 large avocados, peeled
        and mashed
    2 cups light cream
    1 13¾-ounce can chicken broth
    1 tablespoon lemon juice

Advance preparation: In blender container combine all ingredients, ½ teaspoon salt, and dash pepper. Cover; blend till smooth. Refrigerate 5 to 24 hours.
Before serving: If desired, garnish each serving with dried dillweed. Serves 8 to 10.

Festive Cheese Ball

    2 5-ounce jars process cheese spread
        with smoke flavor
    2 3-ounce packages cream cheese
    1 5-ounce jar sharp process
        American cheese spread
    2 teaspoons grated onion
    ½ teaspoon Worcestershire sauce
    ½ cup snipped parsley
        Assorted crackers

Advance preparation: In small mixer bowl combine first 5 ingredients; beat with electric mixer till smooth. Shape into a ball. Roll in parsley. Refrigerate up to 24 hours. Serve with crackers.

Tomato-Cucumber Marinade

    2 medium tomatoes, sliced
    1 medium cucumber, peeled and
        thinly sliced (1¼ cups)
    ½ medium onion, thinly sliced and
        separated into rings (1 cup)
            • • •
    ½ cup salad oil
    ¼ cup vinegar
    1 teaspoon salt
    1 teaspoon dried basil, crushed
    1 teaspoon dried tarragon, crushed
    ⅛ teaspoon pepper
        Lettuce

Advance preparation: Layer tomatoes, cucumber, and onion in shallow glass dish. Combine oil, vinegar, salt, basil, tarragon, and pepper; beat well with rotary or electric beater. Pour mixture over vegetables. Cover; refrigerate for 5 to 24 hours.
Before serving: Drain vegetables, reserving marinade. Arrange marinated vegetables in lettuce-lined bowl. Pass reserved marinade. Makes 6 servings.

Citrus Dressing

Advance preparation: In saucepan combine 1 beaten egg; *half* of a 6-ounce can frozen grapefruit-orange juice concentrate, thawed (⅓ cup); ¼ cup water; and 3 tablespoons sugar. Cook and stir over low heat till thickened. Chill. Fold in ½ cup frozen whipped dessert topping, thawed, and ¼ cup mayonnaise. Refrigerate up to 24 hours. Serve over fruit salads. Makes 1½ cups.

Mealmates that wait

Serve make-ahead Tomato-Cucumber Marinade, → Fruited Granola *(see recipe, page 31), and* Layered Gelatin Parfaits *(see recipe, page 32) frequently.*

Berry-Fruit Freeze

> 2 3-ounce packages cream cheese,
>   softened
> 2 tablespoons sugar
> 2 tablespoons mayonnaise
> 1 16-ounce can whole cranberry sauce
> 1 8¾-ounce can crushed pineapple,
>   drained
> ½ cup chopped walnuts
> 1 cup whipping cream
> 4 drops red food coloring

Advance preparation: Beat cream cheese with sugar and mayonnaise. Stir in cranberry sauce, pineapple, and nuts. Whip cream; fold whipped cream and food coloring into cranberry mixture. Pour into 8½x4½x2½-inch loaf dish. Freeze till firm.
Before serving: Let salad stand at room temperature for 10 to 15 minutes. Unmold; slice to serve. Makes 8 to 10 servings.

Frosty Fruit Salad

Advance preparation: Drain one 8¾-ounce can fruit cocktail. Stir together fruit cocktail, one 8-ounce carton strawberry yogurt, ¼ cup sugar, and 2 tablespoons chopped pecans. Spoon mixture into four ½-cup molds. Freeze till firm.
Before serving: Let stand 10 minutes at room temperature. Unmold onto lettuce-lined plates. Makes 4 servings.

Marinated Cucumbers

> 1 8-ounce carton plain yogurt
> 2 tablespoons vinegar
> 1 tablespoon sugar
> 1 tablespoon grated onion
> 4 cups thinly sliced cucumber
> 2 tablespoons snipped parsley

Advance preparation: In bowl blend together yogurt, vinegar, sugar, onion, and 1 teaspoon salt; fold in thinly sliced cucumber. Cover; refrigerate up to 24 hours.
Before serving: Sprinkle with the snipped parsley. Makes 6 to 8 servings.

Italian Macaroni Salad
A great alternate for potato salad—

> 1¼ cups tiny shell macaroni
>   (4 ounces)
> ¼ cup Italian salad dressing
>   • • •
> 1 cup cream-style cottage cheese
> 1 cup dairy sour cream
> ½ cup chopped celery
> ¼ cup chopped green pepper
> 1 hard-cooked egg, chopped
> 2 tablespoons milk
> 1 tablespoon sliced green onion
>   with tops
> ½ teaspoon salt

Advance preparation: Cook macaroni according to package directions; drain well. While still hot, toss macaroni with Italian salad dressing; let stand 30 minutes. Stir in cottage cheese, sour cream, chopped celery, chopped green pepper, chopped egg, milk, green onion, and salt; chill thoroughly. Makes 6 servings.

Bean Trio Salad
Take this along on your next picnic—

> 1 16-ounce can red kidney beans,
>   drained and rinsed
> 1 15-ounce can great northern beans,
>   drained and rinsed
> 1 15-ounce can garbanzo beans,
>   drained and rinsed
> ¼ cup chopped green onion
> 2 cloves garlic, minced
> 2 tablespoons snipped parsley
>   • • •
> ½ cup olive oil
> ½ cup wine vinegar
> 1½ teaspoons salt
>   Dash freshly ground pepper

Advance preparation: Combine kidney beans, great northern beans, garbanzo beans, onion, garlic, and parsley. Combine olive oil, wine vinegar, salt, and pepper; pour over beans. Toss gently. Chill thoroughly.
Before serving: Drain bean mixture well. Makes 6 to 8 servings.

Marinated Vegetable Bowl

3 medium zucchini, bias-sliced
 ¼ inch thick (about 4 cups)
2 medium tomatoes, cut in wedges
 and seeded
1 small head cauliflower, broken
 into flowerets
½ cup salad oil
⅓ cup vinegar
1 envelope Italian cheese salad
 dressing mix

Advance preparation: In large bowl combine zucchini, tomatoes, and cauliflower. In screw-top jar combine remaining ingredients; cover and shake vigorously. Pour over vegetables; stir gently. Cover; refrigerate for at least several hours.
Before serving: Drain vegetables. Serves 8.

Zesty Vegetable Salad

3 medium turnips, peeled and sliced
 (2 cups)
2 cups water
3 medium carrots, sliced (1½ cups)
½ small cauliflower, broken into
 flowerets (1½ cups)
1 small green pepper, cut in strips
 (½ cup)
1 teaspoon salt
 • • •
½ cup vinegar
⅓ cup sugar
¼ cup salad oil
2 teaspoons curry powder
1 teaspoon salt
¼ teaspoon pepper

Advance preparation: Halve turnip slices. In saucepan combine turnips, water, carrots, cauliflower, green pepper, and 1 teaspoon salt. Bring to boiling; cover and simmer till crisp-tender, about 5 minutes. Drain and cool. In screw-top jar combine vinegar, sugar, salad oil, curry powder, 1 teaspoon salt, and pepper. Cover and shake vigorously. Pour curry dressing over vegetables; toss lightly. Chill thoroughly, stirring occasionally. Makes 8 servings.

Spicy Fruit Salad

This attractive salad is shown on page 95—

1 8¾-ounce can pineapple tidbits
1 8½-ounce can pear halves
2 tablespoons lemon juice
2 inches stick cinnamon
6 whole cloves
1 orange, peeled and sectioned
 Lettuce

Advance preparation: In medium saucepan combine undrained pineapple tidbits, undrained pear halves, and lemon juice. Tie stick cinnamon and whole cloves in cheesecloth bag; add to fruit mixture. Bring mixture to a boil. Reduce heat; cover and simmer 8 to 10 minutes, stirring occasionally. Remove from heat. Add orange sections. Cover; refrigerate several hours or overnight, stirring occasionally.
Before serving: Drain fruit mixture. Remove and discard spice bag. Arrange fruit on lettuce-lined plates. Makes 4 servings.

Orange Perfection Salad

Cabbage and celery add crunch—

1 3-ounce package lemon-flavored
 gelatin
2 tablespoons sugar
¼ teaspoon salt
1 cup boiling water
½ cup cold water
½ cup orange juice
1 tablespoon vinegar
1 orange, peeled, sectioned, and
 diced
1 cup shredded cabbage
¼ cup finely chopped celery
 Lettuce

Advance preparation: Dissolve lemon-flavored gelatin, sugar, and salt in boiling water. Add cold water, orange juice, and vinegar; chill till partially set. Fold in diced orange, shredded cabbage, and celery; turn into 3½-cup mold. Chill till firm.
Before serving: Unmold onto lettuce-lined plate. Trim with an orange twist, if desired. Makes 6 servings.

Cranberry Jewel Salad

Cubes of cranberry sauce are the 'jewels'—

    2 3-ounce packages strawberry-
       flavored gelatin
    2 cups boiling water
    1 cup applesauce
    1 8-ounce package cream cheese,
       softened
    1 cup chopped celery
    1 16-ounce can jellied cranberry
       sauce, chilled and cut into
       ½-inch cubes
       Parsley sprigs (optional)

Advance preparation: Dissolve strawberry-flavored gelatin in boiling water; stir in applesauce. Gradually add to softened cream cheese, beating till smooth. Chill mixture till partially set; stir in chopped celery. Gently fold in cranberry cubes. Turn into 6½-cup mold. Chill till firm. **Before serving:** Unmold gelatin salad onto serving plate; garnish with parsley sprigs, if desired. Makes 8 servings.

Green Goddess Molds

A unique molded vegetable salad—

    1 3-ounce package lemon-flavored
       gelatin
    2 chicken bouillon cubes
    1 cup boiling water
    ½ cup cold water
    ½ cup green goddess salad dressing
    1 tablespoon lemon juice
    1 14½-ounce can cut asparagus,
       drained
    ½ cup chopped celery
    2 tablespoons finely chopped green
       pepper

Advance preparation: Dissolve lemon-flavored gelatin and chicken bouillon cubes in boiling water. Add cold water, green goddess salad dressing, and lemon juice, beating with rotary beater till smooth. Chill mixture till partially set. Fold in cut asparagus, celery, and green pepper. Turn mixture into six ½-cup molds. Chill till firm. Makes 6 servings.

Lemon-Blueberry Salad

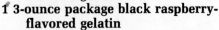

    1 3-ounce package lemon-
       flavored gelatin
    1 3-ounce package black raspberry-
       flavored gelatin
    1 cup boiling water
    1 tablespoon lemon juice
    1 21-ounce can blueberry pie filling
    1 cup dairy sour cream
    ¼ cup sifted powdered sugar

Advance preparation: Dissolve gelatins in boiling water; add juice and ½ cup cold water. Gradually stir into pie filling. Pour into 8x8x2-inch dish; chill till firm. Blend sour cream and sugar. Spread over gelatin. Chill. Serves 8 or 9.

Cottage Cheese-Cucumber Salad

Refreshing salad shown on the cover—

    1 3-ounce package lemon-flavored
       gelatin
    1 cup boiling water
    2 tablespoons lemon juice
    1 teaspoon grated onion
    1 cup cream-style cottage cheese,
       drained
    1 cup finely chopped cucumber

Advance preparation: Dissolve gelatin in water. Add juice and onion. Chill till partially set. Beat till light and fluffy. Fold in cheese and cucumber. Pour into individual molds; chill till firm. Serves 6.

Cottage Potato Salad

Advance preparation: Combine 2 cups cubed cooked potatoes and 2 hard-cooked eggs, chopped. Combine ¼ cup dairy sour cream and 2 tablespoons Italian salad dressing; toss with potato mixture. Combine 2 cups cream-style cottage cheese, ½ cup chopped celery, ⅓ cup sliced radishes, ⅓ cup sliced pitted ripe olives, 3 tablespoons thinly sliced green onion, and ½ teaspoon salt. Toss with potato mixture; pack into 5½-cup ring mold. Chill well. Serves 8.

Succotash Bake

    3 tablespoons all-purpose flour
    1 8-ounce can cream-style corn
    1 3-ounce package cream cheese with
      chives
    1 16-ounce can lima beans, drained
    ½ cup shredded process American
      cheese
    1½ cups soft bread crumbs
    2 tablespoons butter or margarine,
      melted

Advance preparation: In saucepan stir flour into cream-style corn. Add cream cheese with chives; heat and stir till cheese melts and mixture thickens and bubbles. Stir in lima beans and shredded American cheese. Pour into 1-quart casserole. Cover; refrigerate up to 24 hours. Toss bread crumbs with melted butter; wrap and chill. **Before serving:** Bake, covered, at 400° for 30 minutes. Top with crumbs. Bake, uncovered, 20 minutes more. Serves 6.

Broccoli-Blue Cheese Casserole

    2 10-ounce packages frozen chopped
      broccoli
    2 tablespoons butter or margarine
    2 tablespoons all-purpose flour
    1 3-ounce package cream cheese,
      softened
    2 tablespoons crumbled blue cheese
    1 cup milk
    ½ cup crushed rich round crackers
    2 tablespoons butter or margarine,
      melted

Advance preparation: Cook broccoli according to package directions; drain well. In saucepan melt 2 tablespoons butter; stir in flour. Stir in cream cheese and blue cheese. Add milk; cook and stir till bubbly. Stir in broccoli. Pour into 1-quart casserole. Cover; refrigerate up to 24 hours. Toss crushed crackers with 2 tablespoons melted butter; wrap and chill. **Before serving:** Top casserole with crumbs. Bake, covered, at 350° for 45 minutes. Uncover; bake 5 to 10 minutes more. Serves 6.

Fruited Granola

Breakfast or snack treat shown on page 27—

    1½ cups quick-cooking rolled oats
    1 cup coarsely chopped raw peanuts
    1 cup grape nuts cereal
    1 cup snipped mixed dried fruit
    ¼ cup packed brown sugar

Advance preparation: Combine rolled oats, chopped raw peanuts, and cereal. Spread in 15½x10½x1-inch baking pan. Bake at 400° for 10 minutes, stirring once. Stir in dried fruit and brown sugar. Store in tightly covered container. Serve with milk, if desired. Makes about 4½ cups.

Brown-and-Serve Potato Rolls

    5 to 5¼ cups all-purpose flour
    1 envelope active dry yeast
    ½ cup mashed cooked potatoes
    ⅓ cup cooking oil
    ¼ cup sugar

Advance preparation: In large mixer bowl combine *2 cups* of the flour and the yeast. Combine mashed potatoes, oil, sugar, 1½ cups warm water (110°), and 1 teaspoon salt. Add to dry ingredients in mixer bowl. Beat at low speed of electric mixer for ½ minute, scraping sides of bowl constantly. Beat 3 minutes at high speed. By hand, stir in enough of the remaining flour to make a moderately stiff dough.

Turn out on lightly floured surface; knead till smooth, 5 to 8 minutes. Shape into ball. Place in greased bowl; turn once. Cover; let rise in warm place till almost double (45 to 60 minutes). Punch down; turn out on lightly floured surface. Cover; let rest 10 minutes. Shape into 24 rolls. Place on greased baking sheet or in greased muffin pans. Cover; let rise till almost double (30 to 40 minutes). Bake at 325° for 10 to 12 minutes; *do not brown.* Remove from pan; cool. Wrap; freeze. **Before serving:** Unwrap slightly. Thaw at room temperature 10 to 15 minutes. Unwrap. Bake on ungreased baking sheet at 450° till golden, 5 to 10 minutes. Makes 24.

Blueberry-Orange Nut Bread

    3 cups all-purpose flour
    ¾ cup sugar
    3 teaspoons baking powder
    ¼ teaspoon baking soda
    3 eggs
    ½ cup milk
    ½ cup butter or margarine, melted
    1 tablespoon grated orange peel
    ⅔ cup orange juice
    1 cup fresh, frozen, or drained,
        canned blueberries
    ½ cup chopped walnuts

Advance preparation: In mixing bowl stir flour, sugar, baking powder, soda, and 1 teaspoon salt together thoroughly. Beat together eggs, milk, butter, peel, and juice; stir into dry ingredients just till moistened. Fold in berries and nuts. Pour into greased 9x5x3-inch loaf pan. Bake at 350° for 60 to 70 minutes. Remove from pan; cool well. Wrap in foil and store overnight before slicing. Makes 1 loaf.

Layered Gelatin Parfaits

These special parfaits are shown on page 27 —

    1 3-ounce package lemon-flavored
        gelatin
    1 cup boiling water
    1 10-ounce package frozen
        mixed fruit
    ½ cup lemon yogurt
    2 teaspoons sugar

Advanced preparation: Dissolve gelatin and dash salt in boiling water; stir in ¾ cup cold water. Set aside ½ cup mixture. Add frozen fruit to remaining gelatin mixture, stirring carefully to separate fruits. Chill till partially set, 10 to 15 minutes; spoon into 6 parfait glasses. Chill till almost set. Meanwhile, chill the reserved ½ cup gelatin till partially set. Beat with rotary or electric beater till light and fluffy, 1 to 2 minutes. Blend lemon yogurt and sugar; fold into whipped gelatin. Spoon whipped gelatin mixture atop gelatin in parfait glasses. Chill till set. Makes 6 servings.

Rainbow Compote

    ½ cup honey
    2 tablespoons lemon juice
    1 tablespoon finely snipped candied
        ginger (optional)
    1 teaspoon grated orange peel
    4 oranges, peeled and sliced
    2 cups cubed honeydew
    1½ cups halved strawberries
    1½ cups fresh blueberries

Advance preparation: Combine honey, lemon juice, ginger, and orange peel. Pour over oranges in bowl; refrigerate several hours or overnight. Chill remaining fruits.
Before serving: Drain oranges, reserving liquid. Arrange oranges in bottom of compote. Layer honeydew, strawberries, and blueberries atop. Pour reserved liquid over all. Garnish with additional whole strawberries, if desired. Makes 10 servings.

Cranberry-Applesauce-Oat Cake

    1 cup sugar
    ½ cup shortening
    2 eggs
    1 8½-ounce can applesauce (1 cup)
    1¾ cups all-purpose flour
    1 teaspoon ground cinnamon
    ¾ teaspoon baking soda
    ½ teaspoon salt
    ¼ teaspoon ground cloves
    ¼ teaspoon ground nutmeg
    1 cup quick-cooking rolled oats
    1 8-ounce can whole cranberry sauce

Advance preparation: Cream together sugar, shortening, and eggs. Add applesauce; blend well. Stir flour, cinnamon, soda, salt, cloves, and nutmeg together thoroughly. Add to creamed mixture, blending well. Stir in oats and cranberry sauce. Spread evenly in greased and floured 9x9x2-inch baking pan. Bake at 350° for 45 to 50 minutes. Cool in pan 10 minutes; remove and cool thoroughly on rack. Wrap in foil; store in refrigerator at least 1 to 2 days.
Before serving: Cut cake in squares. Top with whipped dessert topping, if desired.

Chocolate Surprise Cake

    1 10-inch angel cake
    32 large marshmallows
    ⅓ cup water
    ¼ teaspoon salt
    1 6-ounce package semisweet
        chocolate pieces (1 cup)
    ¼ teaspoon vanilla
    1 cup whipping cream

Advance preparation: Slice 1 inch off top of angel cake; set aside. Cut down into cake, removing interior; leave a wall 1 inch thick on all sides. Place cake on plate. In medium saucepan combine marshmallows, water, and salt. Cook, stirring constantly, over low heat till marshmallows melt. Add chocolate pieces and vanilla; stir till chocolate melts. Cool mixture to room temperature. Whip cream till soft peaks form; fold in the chocolate mixture. Spoon chocolate-cream mixture into hollowed portion of cake; replace top section of the cake. Refrigerate up to 24 hours.
Before serving: If desired, frost cake with additional whipped cream or sprinkle with powdered sugar. Makes 12 to 16 servings.

Angel Sherbet Supreme

    1 10-inch angel cake
    1 quart pineapple sherbet
    ¼ cup green crème de menthe
    1 cup whipping cream
    2 tablespoons sugar
    2 or 3 drops green food coloring

Advance preparation: Slice 1 inch off top of cake; set aside. Cut down into cake, removing interior; leave a wall 1 inch thick on all sides. Stir sherbet just till softened. Swirl crème de menthe into sherbet; quickly spoon into hollowed portion of cake. Replace top section of cake. Wrap and freeze up to 1 week.
Before serving: Place cake on serving plate. Whip cream, sugar, and food coloring just till soft peaks form. Frost top and sides of cake with whipped cream mixture. Serve immediately. Makes 8 to 10 servings.

Chocolate Swirl Cookies

    1 cup sugar
    ½ cup butter or margarine
    2 eggs
    2 1-ounce squares unsweetened
        chocolate, melted and cooled
    1 teaspoon vanilla
    2 cups all-purpose flour
    1½ teaspoons baking powder
    ½ teaspoon salt
    ½ teaspoon baking soda
    ½ teaspoon ground cinnamon
    ¼ teaspoon ground ginger
    ¼ teaspoon ground allspice
    Sugar

Advance preparation: Cream 1 cup sugar and butter or margarine till light and fluffy. Add eggs, melted chocolate, and vanilla; beat well. Stir flour, baking powder, salt, soda, cinnamon, ginger, and allspice together thoroughly. Stir into creamed mixture; mix well. Chill thoroughly.
Before serving: To form swirls, roll about 2 teaspoons dough on lightly floured board with hands to form a rope about 9 inches long. Place on ungreased cookie sheet and coil into spiral shape. Sprinkle with additional sugar. Bake at 350° for 10 minutes. Makes about 5 dozen cookies.

Chocolate-Marshmallow Pie

    16 large marshmallows
    ½ cup milk
    1 7½-ounce bar milk chocolate with
        almonds, broken into chunks
    1 cup whipping cream
    1 *baked* 9-inch pastry shell

Advance preparation: In top of double boiler combine marshmallows and milk. Place over hot, not boiling water (upper pan should not touch water); stir mixture till marshmallows melt. Add chocolate bar; stir till melted and smooth. Cool to room temperature. Whip cream; fold into marshmallow mixture. Turn into baked pastry shell. Cover with clear plastic wrap. Refrigerate at least 6 hours or overnight.

Chocolate Layer Pie

Advance preparation: Cook one 3¾- or 4-ounce package *regular* chocolate pudding mix according to package directions for pie; cover surface with waxed paper and cool. Prepare one 3⅝- or 3¾-ounce package *instant* vanilla pudding mix according to package directions for pie, *except* use only 1 cup milk and add 1 cup dairy sour cream. Beat *1 cup* of the prepared vanilla pudding into cooled chocolate pudding till smooth. Spread evenly in a *baked* 9-inch pastry shell. Add 2 tablespoons milk to remaining vanilla pudding, beating till smooth. Spread over chocolate filling immediately. Chill till set. Garnish with chocolate curls.

Grasshopper Pie

Chocolate wafers
1 7- or 10-ounce jar marshmallow creme
2 tablespoons green crème de menthe
2 tablespoons white crème de cacao
1 cup whipping cream

Advance preparation: Line 8-inch pie plate with wafers, using half-wafers for sides and filling in spaces with pieces. Combine next 3 ingredients. Beat on high speed of electric mixer for 1 minute. Whip cream; fold into marshmallow mixture. Spoon filling into wafer crust. Freeze 8 hours or overnight (will not freeze solid).

With a Grasshopper Pie in the freezer, can a party be far away? Make the pie several days in advance of mid-week or Friday-night entertaining. Garnish with whipped cream and chocolate curls just before serving.

Creamy Apricot Dessert

1 17-ounce can unpeeled apricot
  halves
2 tablespoons sugar
1 tablespoon cornstarch
½ cup lemon yogurt
2 drops yellow food coloring
1½ cups halved seedless green grapes
¼ cup flaked coconut, toasted

Advance preparation: Drain apricots, reserving syrup. Cut up apricots; set aside. In
saucepan mix sugar and cornstarch; blend
in reserved syrup. Cook and stir till thickened and bubbly; cook and stir 2 to 3 minutes more. Remove from heat; cool to luke-
warm. Stir in yogurt and food coloring. Add
apricots, grapes, and coconut; mix lightly.
Cover; refrigerate 4 to 24 hours.
Before serving: Spoon fruit mixture into
sherbets; garnish with additional toasted
coconut, if desired. Makes 6 servings.

Choco-Mint Freeze

1¼ cups finely crushed vanilla wafers
¼ cup butter or margarine, melted
1 quart peppermint stick ice cream,
  softened
½ cup butter or margarine
2 1-ounce squares unsweetened
  chocolate
3 well-beaten egg yolks
1½ cups sifted powdered sugar
½ cup chopped pecans
1 teaspoon vanilla
3 egg whites

Advance preparation: Toss together crumbs
and ¼ cup melted butter. Reserve ¼ cup
crumb mixture; press remaining crumb
mixture into 9x9x2-inch baking pan. Spread
with ice cream; freeze. Meanwhile, melt
½ cup butter and chocolate over low heat;
gradually stir into yolks with the sugar,
nuts, and vanilla. Cool well. Beat whites
till stiff peaks form. Beat chocolate mixture
till smooth; fold in egg whites. Spread
chocolate mixture over ice cream. Top with
reserved crumbs; freeze. Serves 8.

Is Sifting Necessary?

Sifting flour sometimes seems like an
unnecessary step—often it is. You don't
need to sift all-purpose flour when using
it for general baking. Simply stir the flour
and then spoon it *lightly* into the measuring cup and level off. (Never pack
the flour into the cup.)

  Since cake flour has a greater ten-
dency to pack down, always sift it and
then spoon lightly into the cup.

Sour Cream Pound Cake

2¾ cups sugar
1 cup butter or margarine
6 eggs
3 cups all-purpose flour
¼ teaspoon baking soda
1 cup dairy sour cream
½ teaspoon lemon extract
½ teaspoon orange extract
½ teaspoon vanilla

Advance preparation: In mixer bowl cream
sugar and butter till light and fluffy. Add
eggs one at a time, beating well after each.
Stir flour, soda, and ½ teaspoon salt together thoroughly; add to creamed mixture
alternately with sour cream, beating after
each addition. Add extracts and vanilla;
beat well. Pour into greased and floured
10-inch tube pan. Bake at 350° till done,
about 1½ hours. Cool 15 minutes; remove
from pan. Cool thoroughly. Sprinkle with
powdered sugar, if desired.

Polynesian Parfaits

Advance preparation: Combine one 8-
ounce carton pineapple yogurt, 1 tablespoon sugar, and ⅛ teaspoon ground
nutmeg. Drain one 11-ounce can mandarin
orange sections and one 8¾-ounce can pineapple tidbits well. In parfait glasses layer
yogurt mixture with oranges and pineapple.
Refrigerate up to 24 hours. Serves 4.

In A Jiffy

Last-minute office duties? Traffic jam? Only an hour before you have to leave again? Whatever the reason you're rushed at mealtime, use the recipes in this section to help you get back on schedule.

You'll find cook-at-the-table fondues, elegant stir-fry dishes, hearty omelets, meal-size sandwiches and main dish salads, tasty soups, speedy appetizers, salads, vegetable and bread fix-ups, and quick desserts. In all, there are more than 100 recipes, any one of which you can prepare in 30 minutes or less. That's only half an hour from when you walk into the kitchen until you're ready to eat.

And next time unexpected company drops in at mealtime, you'll appreciate the recipes marked with the entertaining symbol. Your guests will be impressed with the good food and your relaxed manner.

Special Chicken Dinner Omelet *features a tasty filling and creamy sauce. This quick dish starts with eggs, garlic croutons, and chicken à la king. (See recipe, page 48.)*

Main Dishes

Beef-Tomato Skillet

Dry red wine complements the flavor —

> 4 beef cube steaks, cut in strips
> 1 medium onion, sliced and separated
>   into rings
> 2 tablespoons butter or margarine
> • • •
> 1 cup water
> 1 envelope beef-flavored mushroom
>   soup mix
> 1 medium tomato, chopped
> ¼ cup dry red wine
>   Hot cooked noodles

In skillet quickly cook steak strips and onion in butter or margarine till tender. Add water and dry mushroom soup mix; simmer over low heat for 10 minutes. Stir in tomato and wine; heat through. Serve over hot cooked noodles. Makes 4 servings.

Pizza Patties

Crustless pizza with a great flavor —

> 1 beaten egg
> 1 10½-ounce can pizza sauce
> ⅓ cup fine dry bread crumbs
> 2 teaspoons instant minced onion
> ½ teaspoon dried oregano, crushed
> ¼ teaspoon salt
>   Dash pepper
> 1½ pounds ground beef
> 3 slices mozzarella cheese, cut
>   in half

Preheat broiler. In mixing bowl combine egg, ⅓ cup of the pizza sauce, bread crumbs, instant minced onion, oregano, salt, and pepper. Add beef; mix well. Shape mixture into 6 patties. Broil 3 to 4 inches from heat for 15 minutes, turning once and brushing frequently with remaining pizza sauce. Top *each* patty with *half* slice cheese. Broil just till cheese melts. Heat and pass remaining pizza sauce. Serves 6.

Meatball Hot Pot

ENTERTAINING SPECIAL

> ½ pound ground beef
> ¼ teaspoon salt
> ⅛ teaspoon pepper
> 24 ¼-inch cubes sharp natural Cheddar
>   cheese (1½ ounces)
> • • •
> 3 to 4 cups beef broth
> 4 ounces fresh mushrooms, halved
> 1 green pepper, cut in 1-inch cubes
>   Creamy Avocado Sauce
>   Soy-Lime Sauce
>   Bottled barbecue sauce
>   Dijon-style mustard
> 4 cups torn fresh spinach (optional)

Combine ground beef, salt, and pepper. Shape meat around cheese cubes, forming 24 meatballs. Pour beef broth into fondue cooker to no more than ½ capacity or to depth of 2 inches. Heat broth over range till boiling. Transfer cooker to fondue burner. Spear meatballs, mushrooms, and green pepper on fondue forks or bamboo skewers. Cook meatballs in boiling beef broth for 1½ to 2 minutes; mushrooms and green pepper for 3 to 5 minutes. Dip in Creamy Avocado Sauce, Soy-Lime Sauce, barbecue sauce, or mustard. Cook spinach in broth; lift onto plate with tongs. Makes 4 servings.

Creamy Avocado Sauce: Combine one 7¾-ounce can frozen avocado dip, thawed; ½ cup dairy sour cream; 2 teaspoons lemon juice; ¼ teaspoon salt; and dash bottled hot pepper sauce. Makes 1⅓ cups.

Soy-Lime Sauce: Combine ¼ cup soy sauce, 2 tablespoons lime juice, and dash ground ginger. Makes ⅓ cup.

More fondue fun

Beef broth instead of oil is heated in the fondue pot → for Meatball Hot Pot. Sliced crisp vegetables and tiny meatballs are cooked in the boiling broth.

Broiled Meat Loaf

 3 tablespoons milk
 2 tablespoons fine dry bread crumbs
 2 teaspoons finely chopped green
    onion
 2 teaspoons snipped parsley
 ¼ teaspoon Worcestershire sauce
 ¼ teaspoon salt
    Dash ground nutmeg
 ½ pound ground beef
    Mushroom Sauce

Preheat broiler. In mixing bowl combine milk, fine dry bread crumbs, green onion, parsley, Worcestershire sauce, salt, nutmeg, and dash pepper. Add ground beef; mix well. Pat meat mixture into a square about ¾ inch thick. Cut the square in half to form two rectangles. Broil meat rectangles about 4 inches from heat to desired degree of doneness, turning once. (Allow about 5 minutes on each side for medium.) Serve with Mushroom Sauce. Makes 2 servings.

Mushroom Sauce: Drain *half* of a 3-ounce can sliced mushrooms. In small saucepan melt 1 tablespoon butter. Stir in 1 teaspoon all-purpose flour and dash pepper. Add ¼ cup milk all at once. Cook and stir till thickened and bubbly. Stir in drained mushrooms; heat through.

Chili-Hominy Skillet

 1 pound ground beef
 1 16-ounce can yellow hominy,
    drained
 ¼ cup fresh or frozen chopped
    green pepper
 ¼ cup water
 ½ envelope chili seasoning mix
    (2 tablespoons)
 2 tablespoons onion soup mix
 ½ cup shredded natural Cheddar
    cheese (2 ounces)

Brown the beef; drain off fat. Stir in hominy, green pepper, water, chili seasoning, and soup mix. Cook and stir till heated through, about 5 minutes. Sprinkle cheese over; cover and cook till cheese melts. Serves 4.

Dijon-Style Liver

A delicious liver and onion dish—

 ⅓ cup sliced green onion with tops
 2 tablespoons butter or margarine
 ¼ cup all-purpose flour
 ¼ teaspoon salt
    Dash pepper
 1 pound calf's liver, cut ¾ inch
    thick (4 slices)
 1 tablespoon water
 2 teaspoons Dijon-style mustard
 2 teaspoons Worcestershire sauce
 1 teaspoon lemon juice

In skillet cook green onion in 1 *tablespoon* of the butter till tender but not brown; remove from skillet. Combine flour, salt, and pepper; dip liver in flour mixture to coat. In same skillet melt remaining butter. Cook liver in butter over medium heat for 3 minutes. Turn liver; cook 3 minutes more. Remove to warm platter. Return onion to skillet along with water, mustard, Worcestershire, and lemon juice; cook and stir till heated through. Spoon mustard sauce over liver. Makes 4 servings.

Wine-Sauced Hamburger Steak

 ¾ pound lean ground beef
 ½ teaspoon salt
    Dash pepper
    • • •
 1 tablespoon butter or margarine
 2 tablespoons dry red wine
 2 teaspoons dried parsley flakes
 1 teaspoon lemon juice
 ½ teaspoon instant minced onion
 ¼ teaspoon Worcestershire sauce

Combine ground beef, salt, and pepper; mix well. Shape into 2 patties about ½ inch thick. In skillet melt butter. Cook meat to desired doneness, turning once. (Allow 2 minutes on each side for medium-rare.) Remove meat to warm plates. In same skillet combine wine, parsley flakes, lemon juice, instant minced onion, and Worcestershire sauce; heat to boiling. Pour over meat. Makes 2 servings.

Jiffy Steak au Poivre

Flame these at the table—

2 beef cube steaks
1 teaspoon freshly ground pepper
2 tablespoons butter or
      margarine
Salt

• • •

2 tablespoons brandy

Sprinkle beef cube steaks on both sides
with freshly ground pepper, pressing in
firmly with hands. In medium skillet brown
the steaks very quickly in butter or margarine, about 1 minute on each side. Sprinkle
with salt. Add brandy to skillet; flame. Remove steaks to warm serving platter; pour
pan drippings over. Makes 2 servings.

Stir-Fry Beef with Asparagus

A perfect use for a wok—

1 pound beef flank steak, partially
      frozen
2 tablespoons soy sauce
1 tablespoon cornstarch
1 tablespoon cooking oil

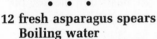

• • •

12 fresh asparagus spears
      Boiling water
3 tablespoons cooking oil
1 teaspoon sugar
2 tablespoons dry sherry
2 tablespoons chicken broth

Using a sharp knife, cut the flank steak
across the grain into very thin slices.
Combine soy sauce, cornstarch, and the 1
tablespoon cooking oil; pour over beef
slices and stir to coat all meat. Cut fresh
asparagus on the bias into 1-inch pieces.
Drop asparagus pieces into pan of boiling
water. Simmer 1 to 2 minutes. Drain well.
Heat the 3 tablespoons cooking oil in skillet
or wok till sizzling. Sprinkle sugar over hot
oil. Add beef strips; cook and stir quickly
for 1 minute. Add asparagus pieces; cook,
stirring constantly, 1 minute more. Stir
in the dry sherry and the chicken broth;
cook ½ minute more. Makes 4 servings.

Planning Menus Saves Time

Spend some time each week planning
the week's menus and your shopping list
(see page 96). Then, buy all the groceries
in one shopping trip. This way, preparation will proceed smoothly because
you'll have everything you need on hand.

Barbecue-Sauced Kabobs

Meat and vegetable kabobs shown on page 4—

½ cup hot-style catsup
2 tablespoons packed brown sugar
1 tablespoon lemon juice
1 tablespoon vinegar
1 teaspoon Worcestershire sauce
1 medium zucchini, cut in 1-inch
      slices and halved (½ pound)
      Cooking oil
1 pound beef sirloin, cut in 1½-
      inch cubes
1 16-ounce can whole white potatoes
      Snipped parsley
      Hot cooked rice

Preheat broiler. Combine first 5 ingredients.
Brush zucchini lightly with oil. On 4 long
skewers alternately thread beef, potatoes,
and zucchini. Brush with catsup mixture.
Broil 4 to 5 inches from heat for about 20
minutes; turn once and brush occasionally
with sauce. Stir parsley into rice. Serve
kabobs on rice. Serves 4.

Curried Shrimp and Peas

1 10½-ounce can condensed cream of
      celery soup
⅔ cup milk
1 teaspoon curry powder
2 4½-ounce cans shrimp, drained
1 8-ounce can peas, drained
      Toast points

In saucepan combine soup, milk, and curry;
heat to boiling. Stir in shrimp and peas;
heat through. Serve over toast. Serves 4.

Cheesy Tuna

3 tablespoons butter or margarine
3 tablespoons all-purpose flour
¼ teaspoon salt
⅛ teaspoon pepper
1¾ cups milk
½ teaspoon Worcestershire sauce
⅓ cup grated Parmesan and Romano
    cheese
1 6½- or 7-ounce can tuna, drained
2 tablespoons chopped canned
    pimiento
Patty shells or toast points

In saucepan melt butter or margarine. Stir in flour, salt, and pepper. Add milk and Worcestershire sauce. Cook over medium heat, stirring constantly, till mixture is thickened and bubbly. Cook and stir 1 minute more. Stir in grated cheese. Cook over low heat till cheese melts, about 1 minute. Stir in tuna and pimiento; heat through. Spoon mixture into baked patty shells or over toast points. Makes 6 servings.

Macaroni-Salmon Skillet

A fix-up for macaroni and cheese mix —

1 7¼- or 8-ounce package macaroni
    and cheese dinner mix
¾ cup milk
2 tablespoons butter or margarine
1 16-ounce can salmon, drained and
    broken into chunks
1 3-ounce can sliced mushrooms
2 teaspoons dried parsley flakes
½ teaspoon paprika
½ teaspoon prepared mustard
1 cup dairy sour cream
2 tablespoons dry white wine

Cook macaroni from dinner mix according to package directions; drain. In skillet combine cooked macaroni, the cheese from dinner mix, milk, and butter or margarine. Stir in salmon, undrained mushrooms, parsley, paprika, and mustard. Simmer, uncovered, for 5 to 10 minutes, stirring occasionally. Stir in sour cream and wine; heat through. Makes 4 or 5 servings.

Scallop Fondue

1 12-ounce package frozen scallops,
    thawed
1 beaten egg
¼ cup milk
⅔ cup fine dry bread crumbs
Cooking oil
Dill Sauce or Zippy Sauce

Halve large scallops. Rinse and drain scallops; pat dry with paper toweling. Mix egg and milk. Mix crumbs, ½ teaspoon salt, and dash pepper. Dip scallops into egg mixture; roll in crumbs. Shake off excess crumbs. Pour oil into metal fondue cooker to no more than ½ capacity or to depth of 2 inches. Heat over range to 375°. Add 1 teaspoon salt. Transfer cooker to fondue burner. Spear scallops with fondue fork; fry in hot oil till browned. Dip in Dill Sauce or Zippy Sauce. Serves 2 or 3.

Dill Sauce: Mix one 8-ounce container sour cream dip with chives, 2 tablespoons milk, 1 teaspoon lemon juice, and ½ teaspoon dried dillweed. Makes 1 cup.

Zippy Sauce: Combine ½ cup chili sauce, 1 tablespoon lemon juice, 1 teaspoon prepared horseradish, 1 teaspoon Worcestershire sauce, and dash bottled hot pepper sauce; mix well. Makes ½ cup.

Herbed Halibut Sauterne

2 fresh or frozen halibut steaks
1 tablespoon fresh or frozen chopped
    onion
2 tablespoons butter or margarine
¼ cup sauterne
2 teaspoons lemon juice
½ teaspoon dried parsley flakes
⅛ teaspoon dried rosemary, crushed

Thaw frozen fish. Preheat broiler. Cook onion in butter till tender. Add next 4 ingredients. Simmer 3 to 4 minutes. Sprinkle fish with salt; brush with wine mixture. Broil 5 to 6 inches from heat for 16 minutes; turn once and brush occasionally with wine mixture. Heat remaining wine mixture; serve over fish. Serves 2.

Saucy Poached Fish

¼ cup dry sherry
1 10¾-ounce can condensed cream of
     mushroom soup
¼ teaspoon dry mustard
4 fresh or frozen halibut steaks
1 3-ounce can sliced mushrooms
2 tablespoons snipped parsley
   Hot cooked rice

In medium skillet gradually stir sherry into soup. Stir in mustard. Bring to boil; reduce heat. Separate frozen fish; place fish in hot soup mixture. Cook, covered, till fish flakes easily, about 10 minutes. Carefully remove fish to warm platter. Drain mushrooms; stir mushrooms and parsley into soup mixture. Heat through; serve over fish and hot cooked rice. Makes 4 servings.

Lazy-Day Lobster Newburg

1⅓ cups light cream
1 envelope white sauce mix
     (enough for 1 cup sauce)
2 beaten egg yolks
1 5-ounce can lobster, drained,
     flaked, and cartilage removed
2 tablespoons dry sherry
   Patty shells or toast points
   Paprika

Gradually blend cream into sauce mix; cook and stir till thickened and bubbly. Stir small amount hot liquid into yolks; return to hot mixture. Cook and stir till bubbly. Stir in lobster and sherry; heat through. Serve in baked patty shells or over toast; sprinkle with paprika. Serves 4.

Bean-Sausage Combo

In saucepan combine one 16- or 18-ounce can baked beans; one 16-ounce can cut green beans, drained; one 8½-ounce can lima beans; and 2 teaspoons instant minced onion. Stir in one 12-ounce package smoked sausage links, bias-cut in pieces. Heat through, stirring occasionally. Serves 4.

Chinese Pork and Vegetables

¼ cup soy sauce
1 tablespoon cornstarch
2 tablespoons cooking oil
1 clove garlic, minced
1 teaspoon grated gingerroot
1 pound lean pork, diced
3 cups chopped Chinese or celery
     cabbage
1 10-ounce package frozen peas,
     thawed
1 medium green pepper, cut in
     thin strips
1 3-ounce can sliced mushrooms,
     drained
2 tablespoons sliced green onion
2 tablespoons dry sherry
   Hot cooked rice

Combine soy sauce, cornstarch, and ½ cup water; set aside. Heat oil in wok or electric skillet. Add garlic, gingerroot, and dash salt; stir-fry at medium heat just till garlic is golden. Turn heat to high; add pork gradually. Stir constantly till browned, 2 to 4 minutes. Season with salt. Add cabbage, peas, green pepper, mushrooms, green onion, and sherry. Cook and stir 1 minute more. Pour soy mixture over vegetables; cook and stir till thickened. Serve over rice. Serves 4 or 5.

Quick Pork Curry

1 tomato, peeled and chopped
¼ cup fresh or frozen chopped onion
1 to 2 teaspoons curry powder
1 tablespoon butter or margarine
1 10½-ounce can condensed golden
     mushroom soup
½ cup milk
1½ to 2 cups cubed cooked pork
1 cup dairy sour cream
   Hot cooked rice

Cook tomato, onion, curry, and ¼ teaspoon salt in butter till onion is tender. Stir in soup and milk. Add pork; simmer 10 minutes. Stir in sour cream; heat through, but *do not boil*. Serve over rice. Serves 4 or 5.

Cheese soup and caraway seed add a new twist to the popular combination of frankfurters and sauerkraut in Frank-Kraut Dinner. For a special touch, slash the frankfurters before placing them atop the sauerkraut.

Frank-Kraut Dinner

- ¼ cup milk
- 1 11-ounce can condensed Cheddar cheese soup
- ½ teaspoon caraway seed
- ½ teaspoon prepared mustard
- 1 27-ounce can sauerkraut, drained
- 1 pound frankfurters (8 to 10)

Preheat oven to 375°. Gradually stir milk into soup till blended; stir in caraway and mustard. Snip sauerkraut; fold into soup mixture. Heat through, stirring often. Turn into 10x6x1½-inch baking dish. Slash frankfurters diagonally at 1-inch intervals; arrange atop casserole. Bake at 375° for 15 to 20 minutes. Makes 4 servings.

Frank-Egg Scramble

- 4 or 5 frankfurters
- 1 tablespoon sugar
- 1 tablespoon soy sauce
- ½ medium onion, sliced and separated into rings
- ½ medium green pepper, cut in ¼-inch-wide strips
- 6 beaten eggs

Slice franks diagonally into ½-inch-wide pieces. In skillet brown the franks. Remove from heat; push to one side. Stir in sugar and soy. Add vegetables. Cook, covered, till vegetables are crisp-tender, about 3 minutes. Pour eggs over. Cook and stir till eggs are set. Makes 4 to 6 servings.

Bacon-Bean Skillet

    2 16-ounce cans pork and beans in
        tomato sauce
    3 spiced peaches, coarsely chopped
    ¼ cup catsup
    2 tablespoons packed brown sugar
    2 teaspoons instant minced onion
    2 teaspoons prepared mustard
    2 teaspoons Worcestershire sauce
    8 slices Canadian-style bacon

In 10-inch skillet combine first 7 ingredients. Cook, uncovered, over medium heat till thick, about 8 minutes, stirring often. Place bacon atop. Cover; cook till bacon is hot, about 4 minutes. Makes 4 servings.

Ham Barbecue

    1 cup cubed fully cooked ham
    1 teaspoon cooking oil
    1 8¾-ounce can pineapple tidbits
    ¼ cup bottled barbecue sauce
    ⅓ cup cold water
   1½ teaspoons cornstarch
    ½ medium green pepper, cut in strips
      Hot cooked rice

Brown the meat lightly in hot oil in skillet. Drain pineapple, reserving syrup. Stir reserved syrup and barbecue sauce into browned meat. Cover; simmer 10 minutes. Blend cold water and cornstarch; stir into meat mixture. Cook and stir till thickened and bubbly. Add pineapple and green pepper. Heat through. Serve over rice. Serves 2.

Microwave Cooking

Microwave ovens are one of the newest timesaving kitchen appliances. They are suited particularly for cooking small quantities of food quickly and for cutting to seconds or minutes the time needed to reheat or defrost foods. Be sure to follow the manufacturer's instructions accompanying your microwave oven.

Apricot-Glazed Ham

    1 8¾-ounce can unpeeled apricot
        halves
    2 tablespoons packed brown sugar
    2 teaspoons vinegar
    1 teaspoon prepared mustard
    ¼ teaspoon ground ginger
    1 1½-pound fully cooked ham slice
    6 maraschino cherries

Drain apricots, reserving 2 tablespoons syrup. Set aside 6 apricot halves; press remaining apricots through sieve. Combine sieved apricots, reserved syrup, brown sugar, vinegar, mustard, and ginger. Trim excess fat from ham; slash remaining fat edges. In skillet cook trimmings till 1 tablespoon fat accumulates. Discard trimmings. Brown the ham slowly on one side in hot fat, about 4 minutes; turn. Place reserved apricot halves atop; spoon apricot mixture over. Cover; cook 5 minutes. Garnish each apricot half with cherry. Serves 6.

Ham Grab Bags

    1 16-ounce can sweet potatoes
    1 16-ounce package ham steaks
        (8 slices)
    1 16-ounce can Italian green beans,
        drained
    1 20-ounce can pie-sliced apples,
        drained
    1 8-ounce can whole cranberry sauce
    ½ teaspoon Dijon-style mustard
    ¼ cup packed brown sugar (optional)

Preheat oven to 400°. Drain sweet potatoes, reserving 1 tablespoon syrup; slice sweet potatoes. On four sheets of heavy foil, layer the ham slices, sweet potatoes, beans, and apples. Combine cranberry sauce, reserved sweet potato syrup, and mustard. Spoon cranberry mixture over ham and vegetables. If desired, sprinkle apple slices and sweet potatoes with brown sugar. Wrap up foil pouches loosely. Place on baking sheet. Bake at 400° till heated through, about 20 minutes. Transfer to serving plates, pouring juices over all. Makes 4 servings.

Ham with Spicy Raisin Sauce

    1 1½-pound fully cooked ham slice,
        cut 1 inch thick
    ½ cup packed brown sugar
    ½ teaspoon dry mustard
    ¼ teaspoon ground ginger
    1 22-ounce can raisin pie filling
    2 tablespoons vinegar
    2 tablespoons water
    ½ teaspoon Worcestershire sauce

Preheat broiler. Slash fat edge of ham. Broil about 3 inches from heat for 14 to 16 minutes, turning once. Meanwhile, in saucepan blend together brown sugar, dry mustard, and ginger. Stir in raisin pie filling, vinegar, water, and Worcestershire sauce; heat to boiling. Serve raisin sauce with ham. Makes 6 servings.

Meat and Rice Skillet

    ½ cup fresh or frozen chopped onion
    ½ cup fresh or frozen chopped green
        pepper
    2 tablespoons cooking oil
            • • •
    1 29-ounce can tomatoes, cut up
    1 12-ounce can luncheon meat, cut
        in cubes
    1¾ cups water
    1 teaspoon paprika
    1 bay leaf
    ½ teaspoon dried thyme, crushed
    ½ teaspoon dried oregano, crushed
    ¼ teaspoon garlic powder
    3 drops bottled hot pepper sauce
        Dash pepper
    1½ cups uncooked packaged precooked
        rice

In large skillet cook onion and green pepper in hot oil till tender. Stir in tomatoes, cubed luncheon meat, water, paprika, bay leaf, thyme, oregano, garlic powder, bottled hot pepper sauce, and pepper. Cover; simmer 15 minutes. Stir in rice. Cover; simmer 2 minutes more. Remove pan from heat; let stand, covered, for 5 minutes. Remove bay leaf before serving. Makes 6 servings.

Speedy Chicken Chasseur

Pick up the fried chicken for this dish on your way home from work—

    2 medium tomatoes, peeled and
        chopped
    1 3-ounce can sliced mushrooms,
        drained
    ⅔ cup dry white wine
    2 tablespoons butter or margarine
    2 chicken bouillon cubes
    1 tablespoon instant minced onion
    1 tablespoon lemon juice
    1 teaspoon sugar
    ¼ teaspoon salt
    ⅛ teaspoon dried oregano, crushed
    2 teaspoons cornstarch
    8 carry-out fried chicken legs

In 10-inch skillet combine chopped tomatoes, mushrooms, *half* the wine, butter or margarine, bouillon, instant minced onion, lemon juice, sugar, salt, and oregano. Bring to a boil; cover and simmer till tomatoes are tender, about 3 minutes. Blend together cornstarch and remaining wine; stir into mixture. Cook, stirring constantly, till thickened and bubbly. Add carry-out fried chicken; simmer till heated through, about 5 minutes. Makes 4 servings.

Turkey Gumbo

A delicious use for leftover turkey—

    1 cup water
    2 tablespoons cornstarch
    1 tablespoon soy sauce
    1 10½-ounce can condensed chicken
        gumbo soup
    2 cups cubed cooked turkey
    2 tablespoons chopped canned
        pimiento
    1 3-ounce can chow mein noodles
        (2¼ cups)

In saucepan combine water, cornstarch, and soy sauce. Stir in chicken gumbo soup. Cook, stirring constantly, till thickened and bubbly. Stir in cubed turkey and chopped pimiento. Heat through. Serve over chow mein noodles. Makes 4 servings.

Oriental Chicken

An especially colorful dish—

    2 cups cubed cooked chicken
    2 cups chicken broth
    1 6-ounce package frozen pea pods
    1 5-ounce can water chestnuts,
        drained and thinly sliced
    2 tablespoons sliced green onion
    ½ teaspoon ground ginger
    ¼ cup cornstarch
    ¼ cup cold water
    3 tablespoons soy sauce
    2 medium tomatoes, cut in wedges
        • • •
    Chow mein noodles, warmed, or
        hot cooked rice

In skillet or wok combine chicken, chicken broth, pea pods, water chestnuts, green onion, and ginger; heat to boiling. Combine cornstarch, water, and soy sauce; stir into chicken mixture. Cook and stir till mixture is thickened and bubbly. Add tomato wedges and heat just till hot. Serve on chow mein noodles or cooked rice. Pass additional soy sauce, if desired. Serves 4 or 5.

"Ole!" is what they'll say after sampling this Mexi-Chicken Skillet. Canned chili peppers and tamales in it account for its south-of-the-border name.

Blender Tips

The blender can shave precious minutes from many food preparation tasks. For example, use it to crush crackers, make bread crumbs, chop vegetables, combine ingredients for sauces and salad dressings, and blend beverages.

Creamed Turkey Especial

    1½ teaspoons instant chicken
        bouillon granules
    1 cup boiling water
    1 cup light cream
    2 packages white sauce mix (each
        enough for 1 cup sauce)
    1½ cups cubed cooked turkey
    1 8-ounce can water chestnuts,
        drained and sliced
    ¼ cup dry sherry
    2 tablespoons finely snipped parsley
    3 English muffins, split and toasted
        Paprika

Dissolve bouillon in boiling water. Add cream. Prepare sauce mix according to package directions, *except* use cream mixture in place of liquid called for. Stir in turkey, water chestnuts, sherry, and parsley; heat through. Spoon over English muffin halves. Sprinkle with paprika. Makes 6 servings.

Mexi-Chicken Skillet

In skillet combine 2 cups cubed cooked chicken; one 11-ounce can condensed Cheddar cheese soup; one 8-ounce can tomatoes, cut up; ½ cup uncooked packaged precooked rice; and 2 tablespoons chopped canned green chili peppers. Drain sauce from one 15-ounce can tamales and add sauce to chicken mixture. Cover; simmer 5 minutes over low heat. Meanwhile, remove husks from tamales; cut tamales in 1-inch pieces. Place pieces atop chicken mixture. Cover; cook over low heat till tamales are heated through, about 10 minutes. Serves 4.

Chicken Shortcake

Use canned or leftover cooked chicken—

> 1 package refrigerated buttermilk
>   biscuits (10 biscuits)
>   Butter or margarine, melted
> 1 10¾-ounce can condensed cream
>   of mushroom soup
> 1 10½-ounce can condensed cream
>   chicken soup
> ¼ cup milk
> 2 cups cubed cooked chicken
> 1 3-ounce can sliced mushrooms,
>   drained
> ¼ cup chopped green onion
> 1 tablespoon chopped canned pimiento

Preheat oven to 475°. Remove refrigerated
biscuits from package. Flatten biscuits with
hand to make circles about 3 inches in
diameter. Place 5 biscuits on baking sheet;
brush with a little melted butter or margarine. Top each biscuit with another biscuit.
Press edges together. Bake at 475° till
browned, 7 to 8 minutes. Meanwhile, in
large saucepan blend mushroom soup,
chicken soup, and milk. Add cubed chicken,
mushrooms, green onion, and pimiento.
Cook over low heat, stirring occasionally,
till heated through. To serve, separate double biscuits; place bottom half on plate.
Pour on some chicken sauce; add top biscuit
and pour more sauce over. Serves 5.

Chicken Livers Stroganoff

An unusual dish for two—

> 1 cup thinly sliced onion
> 2 tablespoons butter or margarine
> 4 ounces chicken livers, halved
> 1½ teaspoons paprika
> ½ cup dairy sour cream
>   Hot cooked noodles

Cook onion in butter till tender. Add
chicken livers. Season with paprika, ¼ teaspoon salt, and dash pepper. Slowly brown
the livers. Cover and cook over low heat till
livers are tender, about 10 minutes. Add
sour cream; heat through, but *do not boil.*
Serve over noodles. Makes 2 servings.

Chicken Dinner Omelet

Crouton-filled omelet shown on page 36—

> 1 10½-ounce can chicken à la king
> 2 tablespoons chopped canned
>   pimiento
> ¼ cup fresh or frozen chopped onion
> ¼ cup chopped celery
> 3 tablespoons butter or margarine
> ½ cup garlic croutons
> 5 slightly beaten eggs
> ½ cup milk
> ½ teaspoon salt

Combine chicken à la king and pimiento;
heat through. Meanwhile, in 10-inch skillet
cook onion and celery in butter till tender.
Add croutons; toss lightly. Remove mixture
from skillet. Combine eggs, milk, and salt;
pour into hot skillet. Cook slowly, lifting
eggs to allow uncooked portion to flow
under. Place vegetable-crouton mixture on
half the omelet; fold over. Tilt pan and roll
omelet onto hot plate. Pour chicken mixture over. Makes 2 or 3 servings.

Sausage and Hashed Brown Omelet

> ½ pound bulk pork sausage
> 2 cups shredded cooked potato
>   (2 medium potatoes)
> ¼ cup fresh or frozen chopped onion
> ¼ cup fresh or frozen chopped green
>   pepper
> 4 eggs
> ¼ cup milk
> ½ cup shredded process American
>   cheese (2 ounces)

In large skillet brown the sausage. Drain
sausage, reserving ¼ cup drippings; set
sausage aside. Return reserved drippings to
skillet. Combine potato, onion, and green
pepper; pat into skillet. Season generously
with salt; sprinkle with pepper. Cook over
low heat till underside is crisp and brown.
Blend eggs, milk, ¼ teaspoon salt, and dash
pepper. Pour over potatoes. Top with cheese
and sausage. Cover; cook over low heat for
6 to 8 minutes. Loosen omelet; cut in wedges
to serve. Makes 4 servings.

Count on canned vegetables, soup, and meatballs to help you put Confetti Meatball Supper *together in a hurry. For extra eye appeal, shape the rice in a ring mold and spoon the meatballs with gravy in the center.*

Confetti Meatball Supper

Keep canned meatballs on hand for this dish—

In skillet combine one 11-ounce can condensed Cheddar cheese soup, ¼ cup catsup, 1 teaspoon instant minced onion, and 1 teaspoon Worcestershire sauce. Heat through. Add two 15-ounce cans meatballs in gravy; simmer till heated through.

Meanwhile, in saucepan combine 2 cups uncooked packaged precooked rice; 2 cups water; one 8½-ounce can mixed vegetables, drained; 2 tablespoons chopped canned pimiento; and ¼ teaspoon salt. Bring to boiling. Cover. Remove from heat; let stand 5 minutes. Press rice mixture lightly into oiled 4½-cup ring mold. Unmold at once onto hot platter. Fill center of rice ring with meatballs and some of the sauce. Pass remaining sauce. Makes 4 to 6 servings.

Indian Pizza

An unusual fix-up for frozen pizza—

- ½ cup fresh or frozen chopped green pepper
- ½ cup fresh or frozen chopped onion
- 1 tablespoon cooking oil
- 2 12-inch frozen cheese pizzas
  Curry powder
- 1 cup chopped cooked chicken
- 1 cup shredded natural mozzarella cheese (4 ounces)

Preheat oven. Cook green pepper and onion in oil till tender. Sprinkle each pizza generously with curry powder. Arrange green pepper, onion, cooked chicken, and mozzarella over each pizza. Sprinkle curry powder over top. Bake according to package directions. Makes 4 to 6 servings.

Corn Rarebit

½ cup fresh or frozen chopped green
    pepper
2 tablespoons fresh or frozen
    chopped onion
2 tablespoons butter or margarine
1 tablespoon all-purpose flour
¼ teaspoon chili powder
1 cup tomato juice
1 8-ounce can whole kernel corn,
    drained
1 cup shredded process American
    cheese (4 ounces)
½ cup sliced pitted ripe olives
    English muffins, split and toasted

In saucepan cook green pepper and onion in butter till tender but not brown. Blend in flour and chili powder. Stir in tomato juice and corn, blending well. Cook, stirring constantly, till thickened. Stir in shredded cheese and olives; cook and stir over low heat till cheese melts. Serve over English muffins. Makes 4 servings.

Speedy Italian Cheese Fondue

1 15½-ounce can meatless spaghetti
    sauce
⅓ cup dry red wine
3 cups shredded process American
    cheese (12 ounces)
1 cup shredded natural mozzarella
    cheese (4 ounces)
2 teaspoons cornstarch
    Italian bread, cut in bite-size
    pieces, each with one crust

In saucepan combine spaghetti sauce and wine; cook over *low* heat just till mixture bubbles. Add American cheese gradually, stirring till melted. Coat mozzarella cheese with cornstarch; add gradually to fondue mixture. Continue to cook and stir over low heat till cheese is melted. Transfer to fondue pot. Place over fondue burner. Spear bread cube with fondue fork; dip in fondue mixture, swirling to coat. (If fondue becomes thick, stir in a little *warmed* wine.) Makes 6 servings.

Guacamole Burgers

Topped with a tasty avocado-tomato mixture —

1 pound ground beef
½ cup crushed corn chips
⅓ cup milk
1 teaspoon Worcestershire sauce
½ teaspoon onion salt
      • • •
1 7¾-ounce can frozen avocado dip,
    thawed
1 tablespoon lemon juice
    Few drops bottled hot pepper sauce
1 small tomato, peeled and chopped
5 hamburger buns, split and toasted

Preheat broiler. Mix together ground beef, crushed corn chips, milk, Worcestershire sauce, and onion salt. Shape into 5 patties. Broil beef patties 3 inches from heat for 6 minutes; turn and broil till done, about 4 minutes more. Meanwhile, combine avocado dip, lemon juice, and hot pepper sauce. Stir in chopped tomato. Place hamburgers on bottom halves of toasted buns; top with avocado mixture. Replace bun tops. Makes 5 sandwiches.

Creamy Beefburgers

Dairy sour cream adds flavor —

1 pound ground beef
¼ cup fresh or frozen chopped onion
1 tablespoon all-purpose flour
¼ teaspoon salt
1 10¾-ounce can condensed vegetable
    soup
½ teaspoon Worcestershire sauce
1 cup dairy sour cream
8 hamburger buns, split and toasted

In skillet cook ground beef and chopped onion till beef is browned and onion is tender; drain off excess fat. Blend flour and salt into beef mixture; add vegetable soup and Worcestershire sauce. Cook, stirring constantly, till mixture is bubbly. Stir in dairy sour cream; heat 1 minute more *(do not boil)*. Spoon beef mixture onto bottom halves of toasted buns; replace tops. Makes 8 sandwiches.

Barbecued Frank Sandwiches

¼ cup fresh or frozen chopped onion
1 tablespoon butter or margarine
4 or 5 frankfurters, thinly sliced
1 cup applesauce
½ cup hot-style catsup
2 tablespoons vinegar
1 tablespoon packed brown sugar
4 or 5 French rolls, split lengthwise, toasted, and buttered

Cook onion in butter till tender. Add next 5 ingredients and ½ teaspoon salt. Simmer, uncovered, 15 to 20 minutes. Serve in French rolls. Makes 4 or 5 sandwiches.

Ham-Avocado Sandwiches

1 tablespoon lemon juice
1 teaspoon prepared horseradish
Dash bottled hot pepper sauce
⅓ cup mayonnaise or salad dressing
1 medium avocado, peeled and pitted
10 slices rye sandwich bread
5 slices natural Swiss cheese
10 slices boiled ham
1 medium tomato, sliced
Lettuce

Combine first 3 ingredients and ¼ teaspoon salt. Fold in mayonnaise. Slice avocado. Atop *each* of 5 slices bread place cheese slice, 2 rolled ham slices, avocado, tomato, and lettuce. Drizzle with mayonnaise mixture. Cover with remaining bread. Makes 5.

Corned Beef Hash Burgers

Preheat broiler. Split and toast 8 onion rolls. Mix one 15-ounce can corned beef hash, ⅓ cup dairy sour cream, 1 tablespoon sweet pickle relish, and 1 teaspoon prepared horseradish. Spread about ¼ cup on bottom half of each roll. Broil 3 to 4 inches from heat till heated through, about 5 minutes. Top *each* sandwich with a slice of tomato and a slice of process American cheese; broil just till cheese melts. Cover with tops of rolls. Makes 8.

Liver Sausage Special
Delicious served cold or grilled —

8 slices Russian rye bread
Bottled mustard sauce
8 slices smoked liver sausage
(4 to 5 ounces)
4 slices process Swiss cheese,
halved lengthwise (4 ounces)
4 green pepper rings
1 8-ounce can sauerkraut, rinsed
and drained
Snipped parsley
Butter or margarine, melted
(optional)

Spread bread with mustard sauce. On *each* of 4 slices bread, place 2 slices liver sausage, 2 pieces cheese, 1 green pepper ring, *one-fourth* of the sauerkraut, and some parsley. Top with remaining bread. Serve cold or brush with butter and grill on both sides. Makes 4 sandwiches.

Puffy Sandwich Omelet
Use beaten egg white for a puffy topping —

1 egg
2 egg yolks
2 slices bacon, crisp-cooked,
drained, and crumbled
1 tablespoon light cream
2 teaspoons butter or margarine
2 slices white bread, toasted and
buttered
2 stiffly beaten egg whites

Preheat oven to 350°. In medium bowl beat together the whole egg, egg yolks, bacon, light cream, dash salt, and dash pepper with a fork till just combined. In small skillet melt butter or margarine. Add egg mixture to the melted butter and cook quickly till egg is set but still glossy. Fold cooked eggs in half; cut into 2 pieces. On baking sheet place *each half* egg mixture on a buttered slice of toast. Cover both sandwiches entirely with stiffly beaten egg whites. Sprinkle with salt and pepper. Bake at 350° just till egg whites are golden, about 10 minutes. Makes 2 sandwiches.

Jiffy Barbecue Boats

½ cup fresh or frozen chopped onion
½ cup sliced celery
2 tablespoons butter or margarine
1 cup catsup
¼ cup packed brown sugar
3 tablespoons vinegar
1 tablespoon prepared mustard
1 tablespoon Worcestershire sauce
1 12-ounce can luncheon meat, cut
    in strips
6 frankfurter buns, split and
    toasted

In skillet cook onion and celery in butter till tender. Stir in catsup, brown sugar, vinegar, mustard, Worcestershire, and ⅓ cup water. Stir in meat. Simmer, uncovered, till heated through, about 15 minutes. Spoon into buns. Makes 6 servings.

A-B-C Club Sandwiches

⅓ cup mayonnaise or salad dressing
2 tablespoons dairy sour cream
1 tablespoon lemon juice
8 slices bacon, crisp-cooked,
    drained, and crumbled
¼ cup finely chopped celery
¼ cup finely chopped radish
1 7½-ounce can crab meat, drained,
    flaked, and cartilage removed
1 medium avocado, seeded, peeled,
    and finely chopped or mashed
¼ teaspoon salt
5 lettuce leaves
15 slices white bread,
    toasted

ENTERTAINING SPECIAL

Combine mayonnaise or salad dressing, sour cream, and lemon juice. Stir bacon, celery, and radish into *half* the mayonnaise mixture. Combine crab, avocado, salt, and remaining mayonnaise mixture. Place lettuce leaves on 5 slices toast. Top *each* with some bacon mixture, then another slice toast. Spread on some crab mixture and top with another slice toast. Secure each sandwich with wooden picks; cut into triangles. Makes 5 sandwiches.

Peanut Butter Wiches

A tasty variation of the all-time favorite, peanut butter and jelly sandwich—

½ cup chunk-style peanut butter
1 small carrot, shredded (¼ cup)
2 tablespoons orange marmalade
8 slices raisin or whole wheat bread

Combine peanut butter, shredded carrot, and orange marmalade. Spread peanut butter mixture on 4 slices bread. Top with remaining bread. Makes 4 sandwiches.

Taco Burgers

1 pound ground beef
1 16-ounce can tomatoes, cut up
1 envelope taco seasoning mix
6 hamburger buns, split and toasted
1 cup shredded natural Cheddar
    cheese (4 ounces)
2 cups shredded lettuce

Brown the beef till crumbly; drain off fat. Add tomatoes and taco seasoning mix. Stir well. Bring to boiling; reduce heat and simmer 10 minutes. Spoon beef mixture over bottom halves of buns. Sprinkle with shredded cheese and lettuce. Cover with tops of buns. Makes 6 sandwiches.

Deviled Ham Sandwiches

A lunch box treat—

4 slices rye bread
    Butter or margarine, softened
1 3-ounce can deviled ham
2 tablespoons sweet pickle relish
1 teaspoon prepared mustard
¼ teaspoon prepared horseradish
    Lettuce

Spread bread with butter. Combine deviled ham, pickle relish, mustard, and horseradish. Spread deviled ham mixture on 2 slices bread. Top with lettuce. (For lunch boxes, pack lettuce and sandwiches separately. Add lettuce when ready to eat.) Top with remaining bread. Makes 2 sandwiches.

Tuna-Tomato Cups

An excellent choice for hot weather menus —

    1 6½- or 7-ounce can tuna, drained
       and flaked
    ½ cup chopped celery
    ⅓ cup chopped green pepper
    2 tablespoons chopped onion
    ½ to 1 teaspoon curry powder
    ½ cup mayonnaise or salad dressing
       • • •
    6 tomatoes
    Lettuce cups

Lightly toss together tuna, celery, green pepper, onion, curry, ¼ teaspoon salt, and dash pepper. Gently stir in mayonnaise. With stem end down, cut each tomato into 6 wedges, *cutting to, but not through,* base of tomato. Spread wedges apart slightly. Sprinkle tomatoes lightly with salt. Fill each tomato with tuna mixture. Place in lettuce cups on platter. Makes 6 servings.

Antipasto Salad

    2 cups torn lettuce
    1 slice process Swiss cheese, cut
       in strips
    4 slices pepperoni (1½ inch diameter)
    3 thin slices cooked roast beef,
       cut in strips
    1 thin slice fully cooked ham, cut
       in strips
    2 tablespoons chopped sweet pickled
       peppers
    3 tablespoons salad oil
    1 tablespoon wine vinegar
    ¼ teaspoon garlic salt
    ¼ teaspoon dried oregano, crushed
    1 tablespoon grated Parmesan cheese

Combine first 6 ingredients. In screw-top jar combine oil, vinegar, garlic salt, oregano, ¼ teaspoon salt, and dash pepper; shake well. Pour over salad. Sprinkle with Parmesan; toss. Serves 1 or 2.

Turn plump, garden-fresh tomatoes into colorful, edible salad bowls for Tuna-Tomato Cups. The tuna filling, delicately flavored with curry, also contains crunchy bits of chopped celery, green pepper, and onion.

Salmon-Potato Salad

Dillweed adds refreshing flavor —

    1 15½-ounce can mayonnaise-style
       potato salad, chilled
    1 7¾-ounce can salmon, chilled,
       drained, and flaked
    ½ cup cream-style cottage cheese
    ¼ cup chopped celery
    ½ teaspoon dried dillweed
      Lettuce cups

Combine chilled potato salad, salmon, cottage cheese, celery, and dillweed; toss lightly to mix. Serve salad in lettuce cups. Makes 3 or 4 servings.

Ham Salad Combo

    1 cup diced fully cooked ham
    1 cup shredded sharp natural Cheddar
       cheese (4 ounces)
    1 8½-ounce can peas, chilled and
       drained (about 1 cup)
      Thousand island dressing
      Lettuce cups

In salad bowl combine ham, shredded cheese, and peas. Toss lightly with enough thousand island dressing to coat. Serve salad in lettuce cups. Makes 3 or 4 servings.

Oyster-Potato Chowder

Complement this soup with crisp crackers —

    1 8-ounce can oysters
      Milk
    2 10½-ounce cans condensed cream of
       potato soup
    2 teaspoons instant minced onion
      Dash white pepper
    2 tablespoons snipped parsley

Drain oysters, reserving liquid. Add milk to reserved liquid to equal 2 cups. In saucepan combine cream of potato soup, milk mixture, instant minced onion, and white pepper. Heat till bubbly. Stir in drained oysters and snipped parsley; heat through. Makes 4 or 5 servings.

Cauliflower-Ham Chowder

A good use for leftover ham —

    1 10-ounce package frozen
       cauliflower
    1 13¾-ounce can chicken broth
    1 cup milk
    1 10½-ounce can condensed cream of
       potato soup
    ¼ cup cold water
    2 tablespoons cornstarch
    ⅛ teaspoon pepper
    1 cup diced fully cooked ham
        • • •
      Snipped parsley

In large saucepan cook cauliflower, covered, in chicken broth till almost tender, about 4 minutes. *(Do not drain.)* Cut up cauliflower. In mixing bowl gradually stir milk into cream of potato soup. Blend together cold water, cornstarch, and pepper; stir into potato soup mixture. Pour over undrained cauliflower; cook, stirring constantly, till thickened and bubbly. Stir in diced ham; heat through. Garnish with snipped parsley. Makes 5 or 6 servings.

Cheesy Tuna Chowder

A fix-up for canned soup —

    1 tablespoon fresh or frozen chopped
       onion
    2 tablespoons butter or margarine
        • • •
    1 11-ounce can condensed Cheddar
       cheese soup
    ½ cup milk
    1 16-ounce can tomatoes, cut up
    1 7-ounce can tuna (water pack),
       broken into chunks
    1 tablespoon snipped parsley
      Dash coarsely ground pepper

In saucepan cook chopped onion in butter or margarine till tender but not brown. Stir in Cheddar cheese soup; gradually blend in milk. Add undrained tomatoes, undrained tuna, snipped parsley, and coarsely ground pepper. Cover and simmer 10 minutes. Makes 4 servings.

Quick Brunswick Stew

1 16-ounce can stewed tomatoes
1 16-ounce can mixed vegetables
1 10½-ounce can chicken à la king
1 5-ounce can boned chicken, cut
    in pieces
1 chicken bouillon cube
1 teaspoon dried parsley flakes

In saucepan combine stewed tomatoes, un-drained mixed vegetables, chicken à la king, chicken, chicken bouillon cube, and parsley flakes. Bring to boiling; reduce heat. Simmer, uncovered, stirring occasionally, for 10 minutes. Makes 3 or 4 servings.

Corn-Chicken Chowder

1 10½-ounce can condensed cream of
    chicken soup
1 10½-ounce can condensed chicken-noodle soup
1 soup can water (1⅓ cups)
1 8¾-ounce can whole kernel corn
½ cup nonfat dry milk powder

In large saucepan combine cream of chicken soup, chicken-noodle soup, water, corn, and milk powder. Heat through over medium heat. Makes 4 servings.

Herbed Tomato-Chicken Soup

1 10¾-ounce can condensed tomato-rice soup
1 cup chicken broth
½ cup water
¼ teaspoon dried basil, crushed
    Bacon-flavored protein bits or
    crisp-cooked bacon, crumbled
    (optional)

In small saucepan combine tomato-rice soup, chicken broth, water, and crushed basil. Heat soup mixture to boiling, stirring occasionally; simmer 2 to 3 minutes. Serve hot soup in mugs or soup bowls. Top with bacon-flavored protein bits or crumbled bacon, if desired. Makes 4 servings.

Corned Beef Chowder

3 cups milk
1 10½-ounce can condensed cream of
    potato soup
1 10-ounce package frozen Brussels
    sprouts, thawed and cut up
    Dash pepper
1 12-ounce can corned beef, broken
    into pieces

In large saucepan blend 1⅓ cups of the milk and potato soup. Stir in Brussels sprouts and pepper. Bring to boiling, stirring occasionally. Reduce heat; simmer till Brussels sprouts are tender, about 15 minutes. Add remaining milk and corned beef. Heat through. Makes 4 or 5 servings.

Spicy Chicken Soup

1 10½-ounce can condensed cream of
    chicken soup
1 soup can water (1⅓ cups)
2 tablespoons orange juice
    Dash ground allspice
    Dash ground cloves
    Dash ground nutmeg
    • • •
    Snipped chives

In saucepan blend together soup, water, and orange juice. Stir in allspice, cloves, and nutmeg. Heat through, stirring occasionally. Serve in mugs; top with snipped chives. Makes 2 or 3 servings.

Cheddar-Chicken Soup

1 11-ounce can condensed Cheddar
    cheese soup
1 10½-ounce can condensed chicken
    with rice soup
½ of a soup can nonfat dry milk
    powder (⅔ cup)
1½ soup cans water (2 cups)

In saucepan combine cheese soup, chicken with rice soup, and milk powder. Stir in water. Heat through. Makes 4 servings.

Side Dishes and Desserts

Cheesy Bean Dip

1 teaspoon instant minced onion
⅓ cup milk
1 15½-ounce can refried beans
1 cup shredded sharp process
    American cheese (4 ounces)
1 tablespoon finely chopped canned
    green chili peppers
Tortilla chips

In saucepan soften onion in milk. Add beans, cheese, and peppers. Cook and stir till heated through. Pour into small chafing dish. Keep warm over candle or chafing-dish burner. (Thin with more milk, if necessary.) Serve with chips. Makes 2 cups.

Cocktail Reubens

36 slices party rye bread
    Thousand island dressing
1 4-ounce package thinly sliced
    corned beef
1 8-ounce can sauerkraut, drained
    and snipped
6 slices process Swiss cheese

Preheat oven to 400°. Spread bread with dressing. Top with beef; cover with sauerkraut. Cut each slice cheese into 6 pieces; place atop appetizers. Bake on baking sheet at 400° till heated through and cheese melts, 6 to 8 minutes. Makes 36.

Garnishing Hints

Perk up any dish by adding a garnish. Use these simple garnishes for main dishes — sliced tomato, olives, or green pepper, cheese triangles, or paprika. Garnish desserts with cookie decorations, whipped cream, or chocolate curls.

Yogurt-Dressed Salad

1 cucumber, peeled and seeded
1 green pepper, seeded and cut up
3 green onions, cut up
1 8-ounce carton plain yogurt (1 cup)
1 tablespoon salad oil
2 teaspoons seasoned salt
2 teaspoons lemon juice
1 clove garlic, minced
1 head Boston lettuce
1 bunch watercress
1 cup garlic croutons

Cut up cucumber. Place *half* cucumber, *half* green pepper, and *half* onions in blender container; cover and blend till finely chopped. Pour into mixing bowl. Repeat with remaining cucumber, green pepper, and onions. Stir in yogurt, oil, seasoned salt, lemon juice, and garlic. Tear lettuce and watercress into bite-size pieces; combine with croutons in salad bowl. Toss lightly with enough yogurt mixture to coat. Serves 8.

Curried Pear and Cheese Salad

1 29-ounce can pear halves, chilled
    Lettuce
1½ cups cream-style cottage cheese
¼ cup chopped peanuts
¼ cup raisins
½ teaspoon curry powder

Drain pears; slice lengthwise into quarters. Arrange on 6 lettuce-lined plates. Mix remaining ingredients. Mound cheese mixture onto pear slices. Makes 6 servings.

Jiffy accompaniments

Perk up meals with Zucchini with Walnuts (see recipe, page 60), Toasted Bun Sticks (see recipe, page 61), and Pink Cream Dessert (see recipe, page 65).

Herb Mayonnaise

  1 cup mayonnaise or salad dressing
  2 tablespoons finely chopped onion
  1 clove garlic, minced
  1 tablespoon lemon juice
  1 tablespoon dry sherry
  1 teaspoon Worcestershire sauce
  ½ teaspoon dried mixed salad herbs

Combine mayonnaise, onion, garlic, lemon juice, sherry, Worcestershire, and herbs; mix well. Makes 1¼ cups.

Chili Mayonnaise

Mix 1 cup mayonnaise or salad dressing and ½ cup chili sauce. Makes 1½ cups.

Pink Fruit Dressing

  1 cup mayonnaise or salad dressing
  ⅓ cup cranberry juice cocktail
    Dash salt
  2 tablespoons chopped
    almonds, toasted

Mix mayonnaise or salad dressing, cranberry juice cocktail, and dash salt. Stir in almonds. Makes 1⅓ cups.

Lima Salad

  2 hard-cooked eggs
  1 16-ounce can lima beans, chilled
    and drained
  ½ cup diced celery
  2 tablespoons sweet pickle relish
  ⅓ cup mayonnaise or salad dressing
  2 tablespoons snipped parsley
  2 teaspoons prepared mustard
    Dash bottled hot pepper sauce
    Lettuce cups

Chop one egg. Combine chopped egg, beans, celery, and relish. Blend in mayonnaise, parsley, mustard, hot pepper sauce, and dash salt. Serve in lettuce. Slice remaining egg; use for garnish. Serves 6.

Cran-Appledorf

  1 16-ounce can jellied cranberry
    sauce, chilled
  ¼ cup dairy sour cream
  ¼ cup frozen whipped dessert
    topping, thawed
  2 cups chopped apple
  1 cup sliced celery
  ½ cup chopped walnuts
    Lettuce

Cut jellied cranberry sauce in half; cut half into ¼-inch cubes and set aside. Mash remaining cranberry sauce with fork; fold in sour cream, then whipped topping. Stir in apple, celery, and walnuts. Serve on lettuce-lined plates. Garnish with the cranberry sauce cubes. Makes 6 servings.

Quick Salad Ideas

Add flavor and color to menus by creating an appetizing, quick-to-fix salad. Use the following suggestions as a guide:
• Top a pear half with shredded American or Cheddar cheese.
• Serve slices of tomato and sweet onion with your favorite salad dressing.
• Enhance tossed salads by adding chopped hard-cooked egg; mandarin oranges; raw vegetables such as cauliflower; sliced olives; crumbled bacon or bacon-flavored protein bits; shredded cheese or cheese cubes; leftover cooked vegetables; and/or croutons.
• Fix up bottled salad dressings by mixing them with sour cream or mayonnaise.
• Mix equal amounts of whipped cream and sweet French dressing. Serve with fresh or canned fruit.
• Mound cottage cheese with chives atop tomato halves or slices.
• Serve canned peach or pear halves or pineapple slices with cottage cheese.
• Instead of a salad, serve a relish tray including a variety of raw vegetables, spiced peaches, spiced apple rings, spiced crab apples, pickles, and olives.

Dill-Dressed Chinese Cabbage

½ cup mayonnaise or salad dressing
¼ cup milk
3 tablespoons grated Parmesan cheese
1 tablespoon white wine vinegar
½ teaspoon dried dillweed
⅛ teaspoon garlic powder
Dash salt
Dash pepper
1 small head Chinese cabbage

In small mixing bowl combine mayonnaise or salad dressing, milk, Parmesan, wine vinegar, dillweed, garlic powder, salt, and pepper. Cut cabbage crosswise into thin slices; place on individual salad plates. Spoon mayonnaise mixture over. Serves 4.

Cheese-Sauced Broccoli

2 10-ounce packages frozen broccoli
spears
½ cup mayonnaise or salad dressing
¼ cup shredded sharp process
American cheese (1 ounce)
1 tablespoon milk

Cook broccoli according to package directions; drain. Meanwhile, in saucepan combine mayonnaise or salad dressing, shredded cheese, and milk; cook and stir over low heat till cheese melts. Serve cheese sauce over cooked broccoli. Serves 6 to 8.

Swiss-Dill Sauce

Dress up cauliflower, asparagus, broccoli, or carrots with this delicious sauce —

½ cup shredded process Swiss cheese
¼ cup mayonnaise or salad dressing
½ cup dairy sour cream
⅛ teaspoon dried dillweed

In saucepan combine Swiss cheese and mayonnaise. Cook and stir over low heat till cheese melts. (If necessary, beat smooth with rotary beater.) Stir in sour cream and dillweed; heat through *(do not boil).* Serve over cooked vegetables. Makes 1 cup.

Stir-Fried Green Beans

1 tablespoon cooking oil
1 9-ounce package frozen green
beans, thawed
1 chicken bouillon cube
¼ cup boiling water
2 tablespoons sliced green onion
¼ teaspoon salt
1 tablespoon cold water
1 teaspoon cornstarch

Heat cooking oil in 10-inch skillet or a wok. Add thawed green beans and cook, stirring frequently, for 3 minutes. Dissolve chicken bouillon cube in boiling water. Add to beans with sliced green onion and salt. Cover; cook over medium heat till beans are crisp-tender, 3 to 5 minutes. Blend cold water and cornstarch; add to beans. Cook, stirring constantly, till vegetables are coated. Makes 4 servings.

Parsley Butter

Try this on beans, carrots, peas, or corn —

½ cup butter or margarine, softened
2 tablespoons finely snipped parsley
1 teaspoon snipped chives
½ teaspoon lemon juice

Whip together butter or margarine, parsley, snipped chives, and lemon juice. Serve on cooked vegetables. Makes ½ cup.

Curried Cheese Sauce

Delicious served over broccoli or asparagus —

¼ cup milk
1 11-ounce can condensed Cheddar
cheese soup
¼ teaspoon curry powder
2 tablespoons slivered almonds,
toasted

In small saucepan gradually stir milk into cheese soup; stir in curry powder. Cook and stir till heated through. Serve over cooked vegetables; sprinkle with toasted almonds. Makes 1½ cups sauce.

Deviled Green Beans

1 8-ounce can cut green beans
1½ teaspoons butter or margarine
1 teaspoon prepared mustard
¼ teaspoon Worcestershire sauce
   Dash salt
   Dash pepper
   Cornflake crumbs

Heat beans; drain. Add butter or margarine, mustard, Worcestershire sauce, salt, and pepper; stir gently till blended. Sprinkle with cornflake crumbs. Makes 2 servings.

Quick Glazed Sweet Potatoes

⅓ cup water
¼ cup packed brown sugar
3 tablespoons butter or margarine
1 tablespoon orange-flavored
   breakfast drink powder
1 17-ounce can sweet potatoes,
   drained
   Snipped parsley (optional)

In medium skillet combine water, brown sugar, butter or margarine, and drink powder. Cook and stir till bubbly. Add sweet potatoes; cook, uncovered, over medium heat about 10 minutes, turning to glaze all sides of potatoes. Sprinkle with parsley, if desired. Makes 4 servings.

Creamy Skillet Potatoes

2 tablespoons butter or margarine
2 tablespoons sliced green onion
   with tops
1 15- or 16-ounce can sliced
   potatoes, drained
⅓ cup shredded process Swiss cheese
3 tablespoons milk

In medium skillet melt butter or margarine. Add green onion; cook and stir till tender but not brown. Add potatoes and Swiss cheese. Cook and stir gently till cheese melts, 2 to 3 minutes. Blend in milk; heat through. Makes 3 or 4 servings.

Green Bean Succotash

¼ cup fresh or frozen chopped onion
¼ cup fresh or frozen chopped
   green pepper
2 tablespoons butter or margarine
1 16-ounce can French-style green
   beans, drained
1 16-ounce can whole kernel corn,
   drained

Cook onion and green pepper in butter till tender but not brown. Add beans and corn. Season with salt and pepper. Cover; heat through. Garnish with green pepper rings, if desired. Makes 8 servings.

Pea Pods with Mushrooms

An excellent choice for an oriental menu—

1 7-ounce package frozen pea pods
1 3-ounce can sliced mushrooms,
   drained
2 tablespoons butter or margarine

Cook pea pods in boiling salted water till tender but still crisp. Meanwhile, cook mushrooms in butter. Drain pea pods; combine with mushrooms and butter. Season with salt and pepper. Makes 4 servings.

Zucchini with Walnuts

This unusual dish is shown on page 57—

1 pound zucchini, cut in ½-inch
   slices (about 4 cups)
⅓ cup sliced green onion with tops
2 tablespoons butter or margarine
3 tablespoons dry sherry
½ teaspoon salt
¼ cup coarsely chopped
   walnuts, toasted

In large saucepan combine zucchini, green onion, and butter or margarine. Cook, uncovered, over low heat for 5 minutes. Stir in sherry and salt; cover and cook over low heat till zucchini is tender, 3 to 5 minutes more. Stir in walnuts; serve immediately. Makes 4 or 5 servings.

Sour Cream Potatoes

A quick fix-up for instant potatoes—

> **Packaged instant mashed potatoes
> (enough for 2 servings)**
> **¼ cup dairy sour cream**
> **Milk**
> **1 tablespoon sliced green onion tops**

Prepare instant mashed potatoes according to package directions, *except* omit milk and butter. Stir in dairy sour cream. With fork, beat in enough milk to make fluffy. Sprinkle with green onion tops. Serves 2.

Dilly Bread

A perfect accompaniment for soups—

> **¼ cup butter or margarine, softened**
> **½ teaspoon prepared mustard**
> **¼ teaspoon dried dillweed**
> • • •
> **8 slices French bread**

Preheat broiler. In small mixing bowl combine softened butter or margarine, prepared mustard, and dried dillweed. Spread butter mixture on one side of French bread slices. Place bread slices, buttered side down, on baking sheet. Broil till golden, 1 to 2 minutes. Turn and broil 1 to 2 minutes longer. Makes 8 slices.

Parsley-Onion Bread

> **1 tablespoon instant minced onion**
> **1 tablespoon milk**
> **¼ cup butter or margarine, softened**
> **2 tablespoons snipped parsley**
> • • •
> **8 slices French bread**

Preheat broiler. In small mixing bowl combine instant minced onion and milk. Stir in softened butter or margarine and snipped parsley. Spread butter mixture on one side of French bread slices. Place bread slices, buttered side down, on baking sheet. Broil till golden, 1 to 2 minutes. Turn; broil 1 to 2 minutes more. Makes 8 slices.

Toasted Bun Sticks

Crisp breadsticks shown on page 57—

Preheat oven to 375°. Split 6 frankfurter buns lengthwise. Cut each bun half lengthwise (to make 24 sticks). Place on baking sheet. Brush each breadstick generously with Italian salad dressing, using about 1½ teaspoons for each. Bake at 375° till lightly browned, 10 to 12 minutes. Makes 24.

Herbed Biscuit Ring

> **3 tablespoons butter, softened**
> **1 teaspoon lemon juice**
> **½ teaspoon celery seed**
> **¼ teaspoon dried thyme, crushed**
> **⅛ teaspoon rubbed sage**
> **Dash paprika**
> **1 package refrigerated biscuits
> (10 biscuits)**

Preheat oven to 400°. Blend first 6 ingredients. Separate biscuits; spread tops with butter mixture. In 8 x 1½-inch round baking pan, arrange biscuits, buttered side up, to form ring; overlap slightly. Bake at 400° for 15 to 18 minutes. Serves 10.

Pineapple Brunch Cakes

> **1 3-ounce package cream cheese,
> softened**
> **2 tablespoons sugar**
> **1 egg**
> **¼ teaspoon vanilla**
> **1 8¼-ounce can crushed pineapple,
> well drained**
> **6 English muffins**
> **¼ cup chopped pecans**

Preheat broiler. In small mixer bowl combine cheese and sugar. Beat in egg and vanilla; stir in pineapple. Split muffins; place on baking sheet and toast under broiler. Reduce oven to 375°. Spread pineapple mixture atop muffins, using about 1½ tablespoons mixture for each. Sprinkle with pecans. Bake at 375° for 6 to 8 minutes. Serve warm. Makes 12.

Cheesy Biscuits

Start with refrigerated biscuits —

⅓ cup Neufchâtel cheese spread with
  pimiento (½ of a 5-ounce jar)
2 tablespoons butter or margarine,
  softened
1 package refrigerated biscuits (10)

Preheat oven to 425°. In small mixing bowl combine cheese spread and butter or margarine. Spread biscuits with cheese mixture. Place biscuits on baking sheet. Bake at 425° about 15 minutes. Makes 10 biscuits.

Fruit Cocktail Shortcake

Use frozen pound cake for this jiffy dessert —

8 slices pound cake, cut ½ inch
  thick
1 4-ounce container whipped cream
  cheese
1 17-ounce can fruit cocktail

Spread cake slices with whipped cream cheese. Top *half* the cake slices with undrained fruit cocktail; top with remaining cake slices, cheese side down. Serves 4.

Peach Posies

Garnished with colorful maraschino cherries —

1 16-ounce can peach slices
1 3-ounce package cream cheese,
  softened
¼ cup sifted powdered sugar
• • •
1 8-ounce can date-nut roll
2 tablespoons chopped maraschino
  cherries

Drain peach slices, reserving 2 teaspoons liquid. In small bowl blend softened cream cheese and reserved peach liquid. Stir in powdered sugar; mix well. Cut the date-nut roll into 6 slices. For each serving, place a few peach slices on each date-nut slice. Top with a spoonful of the cream cheese mixture. Garnish with chopped maraschino cherries. Makes 6 servings.

Brandied Strawberry Fondue

An elegant party dessert —

2 10-ounce packages frozen
  strawberries, thawed
¼ cup cornstarch
2 tablespoons sugar
½ cup water
1 4-ounce container whipped cream
  cheese
¼ cup brandy
  Pineapple chunks
  Angel cake, cut in bite-size
  pieces

ENTERTAINING SPECIAL

In saucepan crush strawberries slightly. Combine cornstarch and sugar; blend in water. Add to strawberries. Cook, stirring constantly, till thickened and bubbly. Transfer to fondue pot; place over fondue burner. Add cream cheese, stirring till melted. Gradually stir in brandy. Spear pineapple or cake pieces with fondue fork; dip in fondue, swirling to coat. Serves 6.

Fruit Sauce Fondue

An interesting blend of fruit flavors —

¼ cup sugar
3 tablespoons cornstarch
  Dash salt
¾ cup cold water
½ cup currant jelly
¼ cup orange juice
¼ cup pineapple juice
3 tablespoons lemon juice
3 drops red food coloring (optional)
  Apple slices
  Banana, cut in bite-size pieces

In small saucepan combine sugar, cornstarch, and salt. Blend in cold water; cook, stirring constantly, over medium heat till mixture is thickened and bubbly. Add currant jelly; cook and stir till jelly melts. Stir in orange juice, pineapple juice, lemon juice, and red food coloring. Heat just to boiling. Pour into fondue pot; place over fondue burner. Spear apple or banana with fondue fork; dip in fondue, swirling to coat. Makes 4 to 6 servings.

Eggnog Fondue

An interesting treat for the holiday season—

> 1 3- or 3¼-ounce package *regular*
>   vanilla pudding mix
> 1½ cups eggnog
> 2 tablespoons light rum
>   • • •
>   Angel cake or pound cake, cut
>   in bite-size pieces
>   Bananas, cut in bite-size pieces

In medium saucepan combine vanilla pudding mix and eggnog. Cook, stirring constantly, till mixture thickens and bubbles. Stir in light rum. Transfer pudding mixture to fondue pot. Place over fondue burner. Spear cake or banana pieces with fondue fork; dip in fondue, swirling to coat. (If mixture becomes too thick, stir in a little additional eggnog.) Makes 4 servings.

Burgundy-Cherry Fondue

Use the blender to puree the mixture—

> 1 21-ounce can cherry pie filling
> 3 tablespoons red Burgundy
> 4 teaspoons cornstarch
>   Angel cake, cut in bite-size
>   pieces

In blender container combine cherry pie filling, Burgundy, and cornstarch; cover and blend till mixture is pureed. Pour into saucepan; heat through. Transfer hot cherry mixture to fondue pot; place over fondue burner. Spear angel cake pieces with fondue fork; dip in fondue, swirling to coat. Makes 4 to 6 servings.

Tangy Strawberry Cooler

Yogurt contributes the tang—

> 2 cups plain yogurt
> 1 10-ounce package frozen
>   strawberries, partially thawed

In blender container combine yogurt and strawberries. Cover; blend till foamy. Serve immediately. Makes 2 servings.

Jiffy Desserts

To many people, a meal isn't a meal without dessert. If that's the case with you, end the meal with one of these ideas:

● Fresh fruit with cheese is a delicious meal ending. Try apples, pears, grapes, and other fruit with cheeses such as Gouda, fontina, and Monterey Jack.

● Keep canned puddings on hand as the base for many delicious desserts. Try folding whipped dessert topping, tiny marshmallows, chopped nuts, or pieces of fruit into these puddings. Enhance the flavor of chocolate pudding by stirring in a little instant coffee powder or instant coffee crystals, crushed. Add a few chopped maraschino cherries to canned tapioca pudding. Spoon lemon pudding over slices of pound cake. Fold dairy sour cream into vanilla pudding.

● For quick strawberry shortcake, spoon frozen strawberries, thawed, over pound cake or angel cake slices. Top with whipped dessert topping.

● Fold crushed peanut brittle into whipped dessert topping and serve over pound cake or angel cake slices.

● Coat strawberries, grapes, or fresh pineapple cubes with sour cream or fruit-flavored yogurt. Then, sprinkle with brown sugar and/or flaked coconut.

● Combine orange marmalade and a dash of ground ginger, then drizzle over a mixture of fresh and/or canned fruits.

● Scoop vanilla ice cream onto a brownie and drizzle with chocolate syrup.

● Spoon marshmallow creme onto chocolate ice cream. Then, drizzle with chocolate syrup and top with chopped nuts.

● Layer strawberry ice cream and frozen strawberries, thawed, in parfait glasses.

● Drizzle your favorite liqueur over vanilla ice cream.

● Crumble coconut macaroons atop vanilla or chocolate ice cream. Top with your favorite ice cream topping.

● Spoon a little frozen lemonade concentrate, thawed, over a mixture of blueberries and peach slices.

Frozen strawberries, canned peaches, and vanilla ice cream become company-special Strawberry-Peach Sundae *when you add rum and set aflame.*

Cranberry Jubilee

Subtly flavored with brandy—

 ¼ cup sugar
 2 teaspoons cornstarch
 ½ teaspoon ground cinnamon
 ¼ teaspoon ground nutmeg
   Dash ground cloves
 1 16-ounce can whole cranberry
   sauce
 2 tablespoons water
 ¼ cup brandy
   Vanilla ice cream

In saucepan combine sugar, cornstarch, ground cinnamon, ground nutmeg, and ground cloves. Blend in cranberry sauce and water. Cook, stirring constantly, over medium heat till thickened and bubbly. Stir in 1 *tablespoon* of the brandy. Turn into chafing dish or heatproof bowl. Heat remaining brandy over low heat just till warm; flame and pour over cranberry mixture. Blend brandy into sauce; serve immediately over vanilla ice cream. Makes 2 cups sauce.

Mocha Toffee Parfaits

Crushed toffee bars add crunch to this layered dessert (shown on page 94)—

 1 tablespoon instant coffee crystals
 2 tablespoons milk
 1 18-ounce can vanilla pudding,
   chilled
        • • •
 ½ cup fudge topping
 2 1⅛-ounce chocolate-covered English
   toffee bars, coarsely crushed
   Whipped cream or frozen whipped
   dessert topping, thawed

Dissolve instant coffee crystals in milk. Stir into chilled vanilla pudding. Spoon *half* the pudding mixture into 4 parfait glasses. Top with *half* the fudge topping and *half* the crushed candy. Repeat layers in parfait glasses with remaining pudding mixture and remaining fudge topping. Top parfaits with whipped cream or whipped dessert topping and the remaining crushed candy. Makes 4 servings.

Strawberry-Peach Sundae

An elegant meal finale—

ENTERTAINING SPECIAL

 2 tablespoons sugar
 1 teaspoon cornstarch
 1 10-ounce package frozen
   strawberries, thawed
 1 8¾-ounce can peach slices,
   drained
 ⅓ cup rum
   Vanilla ice cream

In small saucepan combine sugar and cornstarch; gradually stir in *half* the strawberries. Cook, stirring constantly, over medium heat till thickened and bubbly. Remove from heat. Stir in remaining strawberries and drained peach slices. Heat rum in ladle or small pan; flame and pour over fruit mixture. Serve over vanilla ice cream. Makes about 1½ cups sauce.

Coffee-Banana Smoothee

An interesting flavor blend—

½ cup light cream
2 ripe bananas, cut up
1 cup coffee ice cream, softened
1 tablespoon sugar
1 tablespoon instant coffee crystals
1 or 2 drops almond extract

Pour light cream into blender container; add cut up bananas, ice cream, sugar, instant coffee crystals, and almond extract. Cover blender; blend at high speed till mixture is thick and fluffy, a few seconds. Pour mixture into 2 or 3 chilled glasses. Serve immediately. Makes 2 or 3 servings.

Banana-Pineapple Shakes

A dessert you drink—

1 cup milk
2 small ripe bananas, cut up
½ of a 6-ounce can frozen pineapple
    juice concentrate, thawed (⅓ cup)
1 pint vanilla ice cream, softened

In blender container combine milk, bananas, and pineapple concentrate. Cover; blend till smooth. Add softened vanilla ice cream. Cover; blend just till smooth, a few seconds. Serve immediately. Serves 2 or 3.

Speedy Strawberry Parfaits

1 8-ounce carton plain yogurt
    (1 cup)
1 3-ounce package cream cheese,
    softened
¼ cup sugar
        • • •
1 21-ounce can strawberry pie
    filling
2 tablespoons chopped almonds,
    toasted

In small mixer bowl beat together yogurt, cheese, and sugar till smooth. In 6 parfait glasses alternately layer pie filling and yogurt mixture. Top with almonds. Serves 6.

Strawberry-Cheese Topping

Fruit-filled cake topping shown on the cover—

½ cup strawberry yogurt
1 4-ounce container whipped cream
    cheese
¼ cup sugar
1 cup fresh strawberries, halved
    Angel cake or pound cake

Stir yogurt into cream cheese till smooth. Stir in sugar. Fold in strawberries. Serve over cake slices. Makes 6 to 8 servings.

Pink Cream Dessert

Ice cream delicacy shown on page 57—

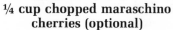

1 quart vanilla ice cream
⅓ cup crème d'almond
3 tablespoons crème de
    cacao
¼ cup chopped maraschino
    cherries (optional)

Spoon vanilla ice cream into blender container. Add crème d'almond and crème de cacao. Cover; blend just till smooth, a few seconds. Stir in chopped maraschino cherries, if desired. Pour mixture into dessert glasses. Serve immediately. Serves 4.

Butter-Rum Sundae

¼ cup butter or margarine
1 package creamy white frosting
    mix (for 2-layer cake)
2 tablespoons light corn syrup
⅓ cup evaporated milk
½ cup chopped pecans
¼ cup rum
    Vanilla ice cream

In saucepan heat and stir butter or margarine till browned; remove from heat. Blend in *about half* of the creamy white frosting mix and the corn syrup; add remaining frosting mix. Gradually stir in evaporated milk. Cook and stir till heated through. Remove from heat; stir in nuts and rum. Serve over ice cream. Makes 2 cups sauce.

Make It Easy

Do you dread meal preparation time because you're left with no time to relax? If so, start enjoying both. The recipes in this section are simple to prepare and require little attention while cooking. So, once the dish is on to cook, you can sit down and read the paper, have a cocktail, accomplish other tasks, converse with your guests, or leisurely prepare the rest of the meal.

You'll find many old favorites in this section, including spaghetti sauce, stews, soufflés, meat loaves, and custard. In addition, there are dozens of delicious recipes that are sure to become new favorites— baked chicken dishes, skillet meals, oven-roasted ribs, casseroles, baked desserts, and many more.

So, follow the advice given in the title of this section. Make dinner easily and then relax.

Put your oven to good use by roasting easy Orange-Glazed Ribs in it. The orange marmalade-ginger glaze complements the crispy pork spareribs. (See recipe, page 74.)

Main Dishes

Sweet Potato-Turkey Pie

2 tablespoons butter, melted
⅛ teaspoon ground nutmeg
⅛ teaspoon ground allspice
1 17-ounce can sweet potatoes,
    drained and mashed
½ cup fresh or frozen chopped onion
1 tablespoon butter or margarine
2 cups diced cooked turkey
1 10¾-ounce can condensed cream of
    mushroom soup
1 8-ounce can whole kernel corn,
    drained
1 8-ounce can peas, drained
1 small tomato, peeled and diced

Preheat oven to 350°. Beat first 3 ingredients and ¼ teaspoon salt into mashed sweet potatoes. Line a 9-inch pie plate with potato mixture, building up edges ½ inch high. Cook onion in 1 tablespoon butter till almost tender. Stir in turkey, soup, corn, peas, tomato, and ¼ teaspoon salt. Spoon into sweet potato shell. Bake at 350° for 35 minutes. Serves 6.

Baked Turkey Hash

1½ cups coarsely ground cooked turkey
1 cup cubed cooked potato
1 6-ounce can evaporated milk
¼ cup finely snipped parsley
¼ cup fresh or frozen chopped onion
1 teaspoon Worcestershire sauce
¼ teaspoon rubbed sage
¼ cup coarsely crushed saltine
    crackers
1 tablespoon butter, melted

Preheat oven to 350°. Stir together first 7 ingredients, ½ teaspoon salt, and dash pepper. Turn into lightly greased 1-quart casserole. Toss together crackers and butter; sprinkle atop casserole. Bake at 350° till heated through, about 30 minutes. Serves 4.

Chicken with Artichokes

4 medium whole chicken breasts,
    split, skinned, and boned
1 tablespoon cooking oil
    • • •
1 envelope spaghetti sauce mix
1 8-ounce can tomato sauce
½ cup dry sherry
1 3-ounce can sliced mushrooms,
    drained
1 9-ounce package frozen artichoke
    hearts, cooked and drained

Preheat oven to 350°. In skillet brown the chicken in hot oil. Meanwhile, combine sauce mix, tomato sauce, sherry, and ¼ cup water. Simmer 10 minutes; stir in mushrooms. Transfer chicken to 10x6x2-inch baking dish. Arrange artichokes around chicken; spoon sauce mixture over all. Bake, covered, at 350° for 45 minutes. Serves 4.

Chicken Pilaf

Preheat oven to 375°. In skillet brown 4 ready-to-cook chicken pieces in 2 tablespoons butter. Sprinkle with salt; remove from skillet. Cook and stir ⅓ cup long grain rice in skillet drippings till light golden. Add ⅔ cup water, ¼ cup fresh or frozen chopped onion, and 1 chicken bouillon cube; bring to boiling, stirring to dissolve bouillon. Stir in 2 tablespoons raisins and ¼ teaspoon salt. Turn into a 1-quart casserole. Top with browned chicken. Cover; bake at 375° till chicken and rice are tender, about 50 minutes. Serves 2.

Easy main dish

A sweet potato crust and saucy vegetable-turkey →
mixture combine to make Sweet Potato-Turkey Pie.
This entrée bakes in 35 minutes, while you relax.

Chicken-Rice Bake

A serving of this dish is shown on the cover—

 1 2½- to 3-pound ready-to-cook
   broiler-fryer chicken, cut up
 2 tablespoons cooking oil
 1 7½-ounce can tomatoes, cut up
 ⅔ cup uncooked long grain rice
 ½ cup water
 ½ cup chopped celery
 ⅓ cup fresh or frozen chopped onion
 ⅓ cup fresh or frozen chopped green
   pepper
 ¼ teaspoon rubbed sage
   Paprika

Preheat oven to 350°. In skillet brown the chicken in hot oil. Meanwhile, combine undrained tomatoes, rice, water, celery, onion, green pepper, sage, ¾ teaspoon salt, and dash pepper; mix thoroughly. Turn into a 12x7½x2-inch baking dish. Arrange chicken atop rice mixture. Sprinkle with paprika, salt, and pepper. Cover; bake at 350° till chicken is tender, about 1 hour. Serves 4.

Peach-Glazed Chicken

 1 2½- to 3-pound ready-to-cook
   broiler-fryer chicken, cut up
   Paprika
 1 16-ounce can peach halves
 2 tablespoons lemon juice
 2 tablespoons soy sauce
 3 tablespoons butter or margarine
 1 tablespoon cornstarch

Preheat oven to 375°. Arrange chicken in 13x9x2-inch baking pan. Sprinkle with paprika and salt. Drain peaches; reserve ½ cup syrup. Combine reserved syrup, juice, and soy. Set aside 4 peach halves; mash remaining. Add mashed peaches to soy mixture; drizzle over chicken. Dot with butter. Bake, uncovered, at 375° for 45 minutes, basting often with sauce. Place reserved peaches in pan; bake 15 minutes more, basting often. Remove chicken and peaches to platter. Mix cornstarch and 2 tablespoons cold water; stir into pan juices. Cook and stir till thick; serve with chicken. Serves 4.

Cheese-Crumbed Cornish Hens

 2 Rock Cornish game hens, 14 to 16
   ounces each (have meatman split
   hens lengthwise)
 ¼ cup sour cream dip with garlic
 1 cup finely crushed Cheddar cheese
   crackers
 ¼ teaspoon dried thyme, crushed
   Dash pepper

Thaw hens in refrigerator. Preheat oven to 375°. Wash hens and pat dry. Coat well with dip. Mix crackers, thyme, and pepper. Roll hens in crumb mixture. Place, skin side up, in shallow baking pan. Bake at 375° till done, about 45 minutes. Makes 4 servings.

Crab-Stuffed Chicken Breasts

 6 whole chicken breasts,
   skinned and boned
 ½ cup chopped onion
 ½ cup chopped celery
 5 tablespoons butter or margarine
 1 7½-ounce can crab meat, drained,
   flaked, and cartilage removed
 ½ cup herb-seasoned stuffing mix
 5 tablespoons dry white wine
 2 tablespoons all-purpose flour
 ½ teaspoon paprika
 1 envelope hollandaise sauce mix
   (enough for 1 cup sauce)
 ¾ cup milk
 ½ cup shredded process Swiss cheese

ENTERTAINING SPECIAL

Preheat oven to 375°. Pound chicken to flatten. Sprinkle with salt and pepper. Cook onion and celery in *3 tablespoons* butter till tender. Remove from heat; add crab, stuffing mix, and *3 tablespoons* wine; toss. Divide mixture among chicken pieces. Roll up and secure. Combine flour and paprika; coat chicken. Place in 12x7½x2-inch baking dish. Melt remaining butter; drizzle over chicken. Bake, uncovered, at 375° for 1 hour. Transfer to warm platter. Blend sauce mix and milk; cook and stir till thick. Add cheese and remaining wine; stir till cheese melts. Pour some sauce over chicken; pass remaining sauce. Serves 6.

Oven-baked Cheese-Crumbed Cornish Hens get flavor and crispness from coating of sour cream dip and crushed Cheddar cheese crackers. Add color to the serving platter with watercress sprigs and cherry tomatoes.

Baked Italian Chicken

Complete the menu with buttered zucchini, tossed salad, Italian bread, and ice cream—

- ½ cup water
- ½ cup chili sauce
- ½ teaspoon salt
- ½ teaspoon dried oregano, crushed
- ¼ teaspoon celery seed
- ⅛ teaspoon pepper
- 1 2½- to 3-pound ready-to-cook broiler-fryer chicken, cut up
- ½ cup fine dry bread crumbs
- ¼ cup butter or margarine

Preheat oven to 375°. Combine water, chili sauce, salt, oregano, celery seed, and pepper. Dip chicken in sauce mixture; coat skin side with crumbs. In 13x9x2-inch baking dish heat butter in oven till melted. Place chicken, crumb side up, in baking dish; pour on remaining sauce mixture. Bake at 375° till tender, about 1 hour. Serves 4.

Chicken-Wild Rice Skillet

- 1 cup sliced fresh mushrooms
- 1 small onion, sliced
- ½ cup chopped celery
- ¼ cup butter or margarine

• • •

- 2½ cups water
- 1 6-ounce package long grain and wild rice mix
- 8 slices cooked chicken (about 12 ounces)
- 1 14½- or 15-ounce can asparagus spears, drained

In large skillet cook mushrooms, onion, and celery in butter or margarine till vegetables are tender but not brown. Add water and rice mix. Cover and bring to boiling. Reduce heat; simmer 25 minutes. Place chicken atop rice mixture; top with drained asparagus. Cook, covered, till heated through, about 5 minutes. Serves 4.

ENTERTAINING SPECIAL

Cranberry-Wine Glazed Ham

   1 8-ounce can whole cranberry sauce
  ⅓ cup packed brown sugar
  ¼ cup dry red wine
   1 teaspoon prepared mustard
   1 1½-pound canned ham
    Whole cloves

Preheat oven to 325°. In saucepan combine cranberry sauce, brown sugar, wine, and mustard; simmer, uncovered, for 5 minutes. Place ham on rack in shallow baking pan. Score top in diamond pattern; stud with cloves. Bake at 325° till meat thermometer registers 140°, 45 to 50 minutes; brush occasionally with cranberry mixture. Pass the remaining cranberry mixture with the ham. Makes 6 servings.

Apple-Raisin Topped Ham

   1 21-ounce can apple pie filling
  ⅓ cup raisins
  ⅓ cup orange juice
  ¼ cup chopped pecans
   1 tablespoon lemon juice
  ¼ teaspoon ground cinnamon
   1 1½-pound fully cooked ham slice
    (about ¾ inch thick)

Preheat oven to 350°. Combine apple pie filling, raisins, orange juice, chopped pecans, lemon juice, and cinnamon. Turn into 12x7½x2-inch baking dish. Place ham atop. Cover; bake at 350° till heated through, about 40 minutes. Makes 6 servings.

Build Nutrition into Meals

Make meals both exciting and nutritious. Follow the Basic Four Food Groups (see page 98) as guides, but remember not to typecast foods. For instance, use milk in soups and desserts as well as in beverages. Feature fruit as an appetizer or dessert. Include vegetables in main-dish casseroles, salads, and sandwiches.

Ham-Potato Bake

This tasty casserole is shown on page 94—

   2 15- or 16-ounce cans sliced
    potatoes, drained
   2 medium carrots, shredded (1 cup)
  1½ cups cubed fully cooked ham
   1 10¾-ounce can condensed cream
    of mushroom soup
   1 cup shredded sharp process
    American cheese (4 ounces)
  ¼ cup milk
   1 tablespoon instant minced onion
  ⅛ teaspoon pepper
   1 cup soft bread crumbs
   1 tablespoon butter or margarine,
    melted

Preheat oven to 350°. Place *half* the potatoes and *half* the carrots in 2-quart casserole. Combine ham, soup, ½ cup of the cheese, milk, onion, and pepper. Pour *half* of the soup mixture over the potatoes. Repeat layers. Combine crumbs, remaining cheese, and butter; sprinkle over the casserole. Bake at 350° till heated through, about 45 minutes. Serves 4 to 6.

Ham Stuffing Casserole

  ¼ cup fresh or frozen chopped onion
  ¼ cup butter or margarine
   2 cups herb-seasoned stuffing mix
   2 cups diced fully cooked ham
   1 large apple, peeled and chopped
   4 slightly beaten eggs
 1½ cups milk
   1 11-ounce can condensed Cheddar
    cheese soup
  ¼ cup milk

Preheat oven to 350°. In saucepan cook onion in butter till tender; add stuffing mix, ham, and apple. Combine eggs and 1½ cups milk; stir into stuffing mixture. Spoon into 8x8x2-inch baking dish. Bake at 350° for 40 minutes. Let stand 5 minutes; cut in squares. Meanwhile, in saucepan combine cheese soup and ¼ cup milk. Cook and stir over low heat till heated through. Serve over casserole. Makes 6 servings.

Applesauce-Pork Loaf

1 slightly beaten egg
1 cup soft bread crumbs (1¼ slices bread)
1 8½-ounce can applesauce
2 tablespoons fresh or frozen chopped onion
2 teaspoons Dijon-style mustard
1 teaspoon snipped parsley
¼ teaspoon salt
Dash pepper
½ pound bulk pork sausage
½ pound fully cooked ham, ground
1 tablespoon packed brown sugar
1 tablespoon vinegar

Preheat oven to 350°. In bowl combine egg, crumbs, ½ cup applesauce, onion, *1 teaspoon* mustard, parsley, salt, and pepper. Add meats; mix well. Shape into a round loaf 8 inches in diameter in a baking pan. With a spoon, make a depression in top of the loaf. Combine the remaining applesauce, brown sugar, vinegar, and remaining mustard; pour into depression. Bake at 350° for 1 hour. Makes 4 servings.

Pork Steak-Vegetable Bake

4 medium potatoes, peeled and cut lengthwise in ¼-inch slices
1 large carrot, sliced
4 pork steaks, cut ½ inch thick
½ cup water
½ envelope onion soup mix (¼ cup)
2 tablespoons soy sauce

Preheat oven to 350°. Place potatoes and carrot slices in bottom of 12x7½x2-inch baking dish. Trim fat from steaks. In large skillet cook trimmings till about 2 tablespoons fat accumulate; discard trimmings. In hot fat brown the steaks well on both sides. In small saucepan combine water, onion soup mix, and soy sauce; bring to boiling. Spoon *half* of the soup mixture over the potatoes and carrots; top with pork steaks. Spoon remaining soup mixture over. Cover; bake at 350° for 1 hour. Uncover and bake 10 minutes more. Makes 4 servings.

Polynesian Pork Steaks

6 pork steaks
1 4¾-ounce jar strained plums (baby food)
¼ cup flaked coconut
2 tablespoons water
1 tablespoon vinegar
1 tablespoon cooking oil
2 teaspoons soy sauce
½ teaspoon salt
½ teaspoon ground ginger
½ teaspoon grated lemon peel
Dash pepper

Trim fat from steaks. In large skillet cook trimmings till about 2 tablespoons fat accumulate; discard trimmings. Brown the steaks in hot fat. Season steaks generously with salt. Combine plums, coconut, water, vinegar, cooking oil, soy sauce, ½ teaspoon salt, ginger, lemon peel, and pepper; pour over steaks. Cover; simmer till tender, 35 to 40 minutes. Remove meat to warm platter; spoon sauce over. Makes 6 servings.

Pennsylvania Dutch Pork Chops

A tasty skillet dinner for two—

2 pork shoulder chops, cut ½ inch thick
1 8-ounce can sauerkraut, drained, rinsed, and snipped
½ teaspoon caraway seed
¼ cup water
• • •
½ cup applesauce
2 tablespoons fresh or frozen chopped onion
1 tablespoon packed brown sugar

Trim fat from chops. In skillet cook trimmings till about 1 tablespoon fat accumulates; discard trimmings. Brown the chops in hot fat. Remove chops from skillet; drain off fat. Combine sauerkraut and caraway seed in skillet; add water. Place chops atop. Season well with salt and pepper. Combine applesauce, onion, and brown sugar; pile atop chops. Cover; simmer till done, about 35 minutes. Makes 2 servings.

Lean and luscious Cherry-Glazed Pork Chops are an elegant yet easy entrée for the hostess who wants to prepare a special dinner for two after five.

Orange-Glazed Ribs

These flavorful ribs are shown on page 66 —

> **4 pounds pork spareribs**
> **⅔ cup orange marmalade**
> **3 tablespoons soy sauce**
> **2 tablespoons lemon juice**
> **¾ teaspoon ground ginger**

Preheat oven to 450°. Place ribs, meaty side down, in shallow roasting pan. Bake at 450° for 30 minutes. Remove from oven; drain off excess fat. Turn ribs meaty side up. Reduce oven temperature to 350°; continue baking 30 minutes more. Combine marmalade, soy sauce, lemon juice, and ginger; spoon *half* of the sauce over the ribs. Bake 30 minutes more, spooning remaining sauce over occasionally. Garnish with orange slices, if desired. Makes 4 servings.

Cherry-Glazed Pork Chops

> **2 pork chops**
> **¼ cup cherry preserves**
> **1 tablespoon light corn syrup**
> **1 tablespoon red wine vinegar**
> **Dash salt**
> **Dash ground cinnamon**
> **Dash ground nutmeg**
> **Dash ground cloves**
> **1 tablespoon slivered almonds, toasted**

In skillet brown chops on both sides. Drain off fat. Sprinkle chops with a little salt and pepper. Add 1 tablespoon water. Cover; cook over low heat for 30 minutes. Meanwhile, in small saucepan combine preserves, corn syrup, vinegar, dash salt, cinnamon, nutmeg, and cloves. Heat mixture to boiling, stirring frequently. Remove from heat; stir in almonds. Keep warm till ready to use. When chops have cooked 30 minutes, spoon on just enough sauce to glaze; cover and cook till chops are tender, about 15 minutes more, basting once or twice with remaining sauce. Makes 2 servings.

Veal Paprikash

> **2 tablespoons all-purpose flour**
> **½ teaspoon salt**
> **1 pound veal round steak, cut in ¾-inch cubes**
> **2 tablespoons cooking oil**
> **1¼ cups water**
> **1 tablespoon instant minced onion**
> **1 tablespoon paprika**
> **1 5½-ounce package noodles with sour cream sauce mix**
> **¼ cup water**
> **1 tablespoon butter or margarine**
> **1½ teaspoons poppy seed**

Combine flour, salt, and dash pepper. Coat veal with flour mixture. In large skillet slowly brown the veal on all sides in hot oil. Add the 1¼ cups water, onion, and paprika. Cover and cook over low heat till veal is tender, about 45 minutes, stirring occasionally. Blend sauce mix from noodle package with the ¼ cup water. Stir into meat mixture; cook over low heat about 5 minutes more, stirring frequently. Meanwhile, cook noodles according to package directions; drain thoroughly. Toss with butter and poppy seed. Turn noodles onto warm platter; top with veal mixture. Serves 4 or 5.

Spaghetti Sauce

    1 pound ground beef
    ½ pound Italian sausage
    1 28-ounce can tomatoes, cut up
    1 15-ounce can tomato sauce
    1 cup dry red wine
    ¾ cup fresh or frozen chopped onion
    ¼ cup snipped parsley
    1 clove garlic, minced
    1 teaspoon dried oregano, crushed
    ¼ teaspoon dried thyme, crushed
    1 bay leaf
    1 6-ounce can sliced mushrooms,
        drained
      Hot cooked spaghetti

In Dutch oven cook ground beef and sausage till browned; drain off excess fat. Stir in tomatoes, tomato sauce, wine, onion, parsley, garlic, oregano, thyme, and bay leaf. Bring to boiling; simmer, uncovered, for 1 hour, stirring occasionally. Season with salt to taste. Add mushrooms; simmer 15 minutes longer. Remove bay leaf. Serve over hot spaghetti. Makes 6 servings.

Texas Beef Bake

    ¼ pound lean ground beef
    1 8-ounce can tomatoes, cut up
    1 8-ounce can kidney beans, drained
    ¼ cup uncooked packaged precooked
        rice
    ¼ cup fresh or frozen chopped onion
    1 tablespoon fresh or frozen chopped
        green pepper
    ½ teaspoon chili powder
    ¼ teaspoon salt
    ¼ teaspoon garlic salt
    ¼ cup shredded sharp process
        American cheese (1 ounce)

Preheat oven to 350°. Crumble ground beef into a 1-quart casserole. Stir in tomatoes, kidney beans, uncooked rice, onion, green pepper, chili powder, salt, and garlic salt. Cover; bake at 350° for 45 minutes. Stir once during baking. Top with shredded cheese; continue baking till cheese melts, about 3 minutes. Makes 2 servings.

Burger Skillet Stew

Using meatballs rather than stew meat reduces the cooking time for this popular dish—

    1 slightly beaten egg
    ⅓ cup fine dry bread crumbs
    ⅓ cup milk
    1 envelope spaghetti sauce mix
    1 pound ground beef
    2 tablespoons cooking oil
        • • •
    1 10¾-ounce can beef gravy
        (1¼ cups)
    ¼ cup water
    4 medium carrots, cut in 1-inch
        pieces
    1 medium onion, quartered
    ½ cup fresh or frozen chopped green
        pepper

In mixing bowl combine egg, crumbs, milk, and *3 tablespoons* of the dry spaghetti sauce mix; add beef and mix well. Shape into 12 balls; brown in hot oil. Drain off fat. Mix canned gravy, ¼ cup water, and remaining sauce mix. Add to meatballs; add carrots, onion, and green pepper. Simmer, covered, 50 to 60 minutes. Serves 4.

Hamburger-Macaroni Bake

Canned sandwich sauce adds snappy flavor—

    1 7¼-ounce package macaroni and
        cheese dinner mix
    1 pound ground beef
    1 15½-ounce can sandwich sauce
    1 10½-ounce can condensed golden
        mushroom soup
        • • •
    ⅓ cup coarsely crushed rich round
        crackers (8 crackers)

Preheat oven to 350°. Prepare macaroni and cheese mix according to package directions. Meanwhile, brown the ground beef; drain off excess fat. Remove from heat; stir sandwich sauce, golden mushroom soup, and prepared macaroni and cheese into the browned meat. Turn into a 2-quart casserole; sprinkle with cracker crumbs. Bake, uncovered, at 350° for 35 minutes. Serves 6.

Oven Hamburgers

¾ cup soft bread crumbs (1 slice)
1 11-ounce can condensed Cheddar
   cheese soup
1½ pounds lean ground beef
¼ cup chili sauce
2 teaspoons prepared mustard
   Hot cooked noodles

Preheat oven to 350°. Combine crumbs, ½ cup of the soup, and ½ teaspoon salt. Add ground beef and mix well; shape into 6 patties. Place in 11x7½x1½-inch baking pan. Blend together remaining soup, chili sauce, and mustard; pour over patties. Bake, covered, at 350° till done, about 45 minutes. Serve patties on noodles. Stir sauce and spoon over patties. Makes 6 servings.

Beef Oven Stew

For unexpected company, double this recipe and bake in a 2½-quart casserole—

1 beaten egg
2 tablespoons cornmeal
2 teaspoons instant minced onion
½ teaspoon dry mustard
¼ teaspoon chili powder
½ pound ground beef
1 tablespoon cooking oil
2 small potatoes, peeled and
   quartered
2 small carrots, sliced
1 small onion, quartered
2 teaspoons all-purpose flour
1 8-ounce can tomatoes
1 beef bouillon cube

Preheat oven to 350°. Combine egg, cornmeal, instant onion, mustard, chili powder, and ½ teaspoon salt. Add beef; mix well. Shape into 6 balls. Brown in hot oil. Place meatballs in 1½-quart casserole. Add potatoes, carrots, and quartered onion. Sprinkle with salt and pepper. Blend flour into drippings in skillet. Add tomatoes, bouillon cube, and 2 tablespoons water. Cook and stir till bubbly. Pour over meat and vegetables. Cover; bake at 350° till vegetables are tender, about 1 hour. Makes 2 servings.

Meat Loaf Skillet Supper

1 slightly beaten egg
¼ cup fine dry bread crumbs
¼ cup fresh or frozen chopped onion
1 tablespoon snipped parsley
½ teaspoon salt
   Dash pepper
1 pound ground beef
1 tablespoon cooking oil
1 10-ounce package frozen mixed
   vegetables
1 8-ounce can tomatoes, cut up
2 tablespoons all-purpose flour

Combine egg, bread crumbs, onion, parsley, salt, pepper, and ¼ cup water. Add ground meat and mix thoroughly. Shape into a 6x3½-inch loaf. In skillet brown the meat in hot oil. Spoon off excess fat. Add mixed vegetables and tomatoes. Cook, covered, about 45 minutes. Remove meat to serving platter and keep warm. Combine flour and 1 cup cold water; stir into vegetables. Cook and stir till thickened and bubbly. Season to taste. Serve with meat. Makes 4 servings.

Chinese Stew

1½ pounds beef stew meat, cut in
   1-inch cubes
2 tablespoons cornstarch
¼ teaspoon ground ginger
⅛ teaspoon pepper
1 tablespoon cooking oil
2 cups water
1 10½-ounce can condensed golden
   mushroom soup
1 small onion, thinly sliced
2 tablespoons soy sauce
1 small head Chinese cabbage, cut
   in 1-inch cubes (4 cups)
1 8-ounce can bamboo shoots, drained

Coat meat with cornstarch; sprinkle with ginger and pepper. In large skillet brown the meat in hot oil. Combine water, soup, onion, and soy sauce. Add to meat. Cover and simmer till tender, about 1½ hours. Add cabbage and bamboo shoots; cover and simmer 5 to 8 minutes more. Serves 6.

Oriental Stuffed Steaks

1 6-ounce package long
   grain and wild rice mix
1 slightly beaten egg
¼ cup sliced green onion with tops
6 beef strip steaks
¼ to ½ cup bottled teriyaki sauce

Cook rice mix according to package directions till done, about 25 minutes. Cool slightly; stir in egg and onion.

Preheat broiler. Using a sharp knife, cut a pocket in each steak. Stuff with rice mixture. Broil steaks 4 inches from the heat till desired doneness. (Allow 4 to 6 minutes on each side for medium-rare.) Brush often with teriyaki sauce. Garnish with mushrooms and watercress, if desired. Serves 6.

Cheesy Onion Steak

½ pound beef chuck steak, cut ½
   inch thick
2 tablespoons all-purpose flour
2 tablespoons cooking oil
4 slices onion
   Lemon pepper seasoning
¼ cup shredded process American
   cheese (1 ounce)

Cut steak in 2 pieces; coat with mixture of flour and ½ teaspoon salt. Pound to ¼ inch thickness. In skillet brown the steaks slowly in hot oil. Top with onion; sprinkle with lemon pepper. Add ½ cup water. Simmer, covered, till tender, about 45 minutes. Sprinkle cheese over onion. Cover; cook till cheese melts. Makes 2 servings.

Remember elegant Oriental Stuffed Steaks when you need an extraordinary main dish. The thick, juicy strip steaks are stuffed with a long grain and wild rice mixture and then basted with teriyaki sauce while broiling.

Mexican-Style Steak

If you like spicy foods, you'll love this dish —

 1½ **pounds beef round steak, cut in serving-size pieces**
 ⅛ **teaspoon garlic powder**
 2 **tablespoons shortening**
 1 **15-ounce can tamales in sauce**
 1 **10-ounce can enchilada sauce**
 ¼ **cup water**

Pound the round steak on both sides; sprinkle with garlic powder. In skillet brown the steak in hot shortening. Drain off excess fat. Drain tamales, reserving sauce. Unwrap tamales and cut in thirds; set aside. Stir together the reserved tamale sauce, enchilada sauce, and water. Pour over steak in skillet. Cover and simmer over low heat till meat is tender, about 45 minutes. Add tamale pieces and cook 10 minutes longer. Makes 6 servings.

Beef Burgundy

 1½ **pounds beef round steak, cut ¼ inch thick**
 2 **tablespoons all-purpose flour**
 2 **tablespoons butter or margarine**
 ¼ **cup fresh or frozen chopped onion**
 2 **teaspoons snipped parsley**
 1 **small clove garlic, crushed**
 1 **small bay leaf**
 ½ **teaspoon salt**
 Dash pepper
 ½ **cup red Burgundy**
 1 **3-ounce can whole mushrooms, drained**
 Hot cooked noodles

Cut steak into bite-size cubes; shake with flour to coat, being sure all flour is used. In skillet melt butter; brown the meat on all sides. Remove from heat. Add onion, parsley, garlic, bay leaf, salt, and pepper. Stir in wine, mushrooms, and ½ cup water. Heat mixture to boiling. Reduce heat and simmer, covered, till meat is tender, about 1 hour. Remove bay leaf. (If desired, serve Beef Burgundy in chafing dish.) Serve over noodles. Makes 4 servings.

Lemony Lamb Chops

An unusual yet delicious lamb dish —

 6 **lamb shoulder chops, cut ½ inch thick**
 1 **onion, thinly sliced and separated into rings**
 • • •
 1 **22-ounce can lemon pie filling**
 ½ **cup water**
 ¼ **cup vinegar**
 ¼ **cup soy sauce**
 Hot cooked rice

Preheat oven to 350°. Trim fat from lamb chops. In skillet cook trimmings till about 1 tablespoon fat accumulates; discard the trimmings. Brown the chops on both sides in hot fat; season with a little salt and pepper. Transfer chops to a 13x9x2-inch baking dish; top with onion rings. Combine the lemon pie filling, water, vinegar, and soy sauce; pour lemon mixture over lamb. Cover and bake at 350° till chops are tender, about 1 hour. Serve the lamb and sauce with hot cooked rice. Makes 6 servings.

Pepperoni Mac

 1 **4-ounce package sliced pepperoni**
 ¼ **cup fresh or frozen chopped onion**
 ¼ **cup fresh or frozen chopped green pepper**
 1 **15-ounce can macaroni in cheese sauce**
 ¼ **cup shredded natural Cheddar cheese (1 ounce)**
 1 **hard-cooked egg, coarsely chopped**
 ¾ **cup soft bread crumbs (1 slice)**
 1 **tablespoon butter or margarine, melted**

Preheat oven to 350°. In small skillet cook pepperoni, onion, and green pepper till vegetables are tender; drain. Add macaroni in cheese sauce and shredded cheese; carefully fold in egg. Turn into ungreased 1-quart casserole. Toss together crumbs and butter; sprinkle over cheese mixture. Bake, uncovered, at 350° till heated through, 30 to 35 minutes. Makes 4 servings.

Swiss and Frank Pie

A variation of the classic Quiche Lorraine—

   1 unbaked 9-inch pastry shell
  ¼ cup fresh or frozen chopped onion
   1 tablespoon butter or margarine
   2 cups thinly sliced frankfurters
     (5 or 6 frankfurters)
   1 cup shredded process Swiss cheese
     (4 ounces)
     • • •
   3 slightly beaten eggs
 1½ cups milk
   1 teaspoon dry mustard
  ½ teaspoon salt
  ¼ teaspoon ground nutmeg
     Dash pepper

Preheat oven to 450°. Bake pastry shell at 450° just till lightly browned, about 7 minutes. Remove from oven. Reduce oven temperature to 325°. Meanwhile, in a small skillet cook onion in butter or margarine till tender but not brown. Place sliced frankfurters, shredded Swiss cheese, and cooked onion in baked pastry shell. In bowl combine eggs, milk, dry mustard, salt, ground nutmeg, and pepper. Pour egg mixture over frankfurter-cheese mixture. Bake pie at 325° till almost set in the center, 35 to 40 minutes. Let set 10 to 15 minutes before serving. Cut into wedges. Serves 6.

Frank-Macaroni Skillet

 2½ cups water
   1 8-ounce can tomato sauce
   1 envelope spaghetti sauce mix
   1 cup uncooked macaroni (half of a
     7-ounce package)
   4 or 5 frankfurters, cut in 1-inch
     pieces
 1½ teaspoons Worcestershire sauce

In large saucepan combine water, tomato sauce, and spaghetti sauce mix. Bring to boiling; stir in macaroni. Cover and cook over low heat till macaroni is tender, 15 to 20 minutes, stirring frequently. Stir in frankfurters and Worcestershire sauce; cook till heated through. Makes 4 servings.

How to Cook Pasta

Use a large pan filled with plenty of water to cook spaghetti, noodles, macaroni, and other pasta. For 8 ounces of any of these, use at least three quarts of water. For seasoning, add 1 teaspoon salt for each quart of water. To prevent the pasta from sticking together and the water from boiling over, add a teaspoon of cooking oil to the water.

Bring the salted water to a vigorous boil, then add the pasta. (Don't break long spaghetti. Instead dip one end in the water and curl the spaghetti around the pan as it softens.) Keep the water boiling constantly and stir at first to prevent sticking. Cook, uncovered, till the pasta is tender but still firm. Drain immediately when cooked.

Plan to serve 4 or 5 from 8 ounces spaghetti and 8 from 8 ounces noodles.

Glazed Sausage Loaf

Spicy sausage loaf topped with a plum sauce is an enticing combination—

   2 slightly beaten eggs
   1 cup soft rye bread crumbs
  ⅓ cup milk
   2 tablespoons snipped parsley
   2 pounds bulk pork sausage
   1 12-ounce package frozen rice
     pilaf, thawed
   1 8-ounce jar strained plums
     (baby food)
   2 tablespoons sugar
   2 tablespoons lemon juice

Preheat oven to 350°. Combine eggs, rye bread crumbs, milk, and parsley. Add sausage and thawed pilaf; mix well. Shape sausage mixture into a loaf in a shallow baking pan. Bake at 350° for 1 hour. Remove from oven; spoon off excess fat. In small saucepan combine plums, sugar, and lemon juice. Heat till bubbly; brush loaf with plum sauce. Bake 15 minutes more. Pass remaining sauce. Serves 8.

Save Chopping Time

Cut last-minute preparation time by chopping several onions and green peppers at one time, then freezing them. So that you can use them without remeasuring, freeze the chopped vegetables in recipe-size portions, such as ¼ or ½ cup. Use frozen portions within 1 month.

Sausage-Macaroni Skillet

½ pound bulk pork sausage
¼ cup fresh or frozen chopped green
    pepper
2 tablespoons fresh or frozen
    chopped onion
1 8-ounce can tomato sauce
½ cup elbow macaroni
1 teaspoon sugar
¼ to ½ teaspoon chili powder
¼ cup dairy sour cream

In skillet lightly brown the sausage. Add green pepper and onion. Cook till vegetables are tender. Drain off fat. Stir in tomato sauce, macaroni, sugar, chili powder, ¾ cup water, and ¼ teaspoon salt. Cover; simmer till macaroni is done, about 20 minutes. Blend in sour cream. Heat through but *do not boil*. Makes 2 servings.

Sausage-Potato Supper

Using one 4⅝- or 5½-ounce package dry scalloped potato mix, in skillet combine dry potatoes and seasoned sauce mix from the package. Stir in water *to equal total liquid* called for on package. Heat to boiling, stirring occasionally. Reduce heat; simmer, covered, till potatoes are tender, about 30 minutes. Stir in one 16-ounce can sauerkraut, drained. Sprinkle with ½ teaspoon caraway seed. Arrange one 12-ounce package smoked pork sausage links spoke-fashion atop the vegetable mixture. Cover; cook till sausages are heated through, about 10 minutes. Serves 4.

Cheese-Stuffed Manicotti

This tasty pasta dish is shown on the cover—

6 manicotti shells
1½ cups shredded mozzarella cheese
    (6 ounces)
1 cup cream-style cottage cheese
⅓ cup grated Parmesan cheese
2 beaten eggs
¼ cup snipped parsley
1 teaspoon instant minced onion
1 15-ounce can spaghetti sauce with
    mushrooms
⅓ cup water

Preheat oven to 350°. Cook manicotti according to package directions till tender. Drain. Meanwhile, combine ¾ cup mozzarella, the cottage cheese, and Parmesan. Stir in eggs, parsley, and onion. Combine spaghetti sauce and water; pour ⅔ cup sauce mixture into 10x6x2-inch baking dish. Split manicotti shells lengthwise with kitchen shears. Open and fill with cheese mixture, using about ¼ cup for each shell. Close. Arrange in baking dish. Pour remaining sauce over. Sprinkle with remaining mozzarella. Bake, uncovered, at 350° till bubbly and heated through, about 35 minutes. Serves 3.

Swiss Cheese Bake

1 cup shredded process Swiss cheese
    (4 ounces)
1 4½-ounce can deviled ham
1 tablespoon prepared mustard
8 slices white bread, toasted
2 cups milk
4 slightly beaten eggs
1 teaspoon sesame seed

Preheat oven to 325°. Mix cheese, deviled ham, and mustard. Spread mixture on 4 *slices* toast, using about ½ cup for each slice. Top with remaining toast. Quarter sandwiches diagonally; arrange in three rows in 10x6x2-inch baking dish, standing *crust side down*. Beat together milk and eggs; pour over the sandwiches. Sprinkle sesame seed over top. Bake at 325° for 50 to 55 minutes. Makes 5 or 6 servings.

Shrimp-Macaroni Casserole

> 1 7¼- or 8-ounce package macaroni
>   and cheese dinner mix
> ½ cup milk
> 2 10½-ounce cans condensed cream of
>   chicken soup
> 2 4½-ounce cans shrimp, drained
> ½ teaspoon Worcestershire sauce
> ½ cup bite-size shredded rice squares,
>   coarsely crushed
> 1 tablespoon butter or margarine,
>   melted

Preheat oven to 350°. Prepare macaroni and cheese mix according to package directions, *except* use the ½ cup milk. Stir in soup, shrimp, Worcestershire, and dash pepper. Turn into 2-quart casserole. Toss together crushed cereal and melted butter or margarine. Sprinkle over casserole. Bake at 350° about 45 minutes. Makes 6 servings.

Combine convenience foods in Shrimp-Macaroni Casserole. *This pantry-shelf special uses macaroni and cheese mix and canned soup and shrimp.*

Cheese-Mushroom Soufflé

> 2 tablespoons butter or margarine
> 1 cup shredded sharp process
>   American cheese (4 ounces)
> 1 10¾-ounce can condensed cream
>   of mushroom soup
> 1½ cups soft bread crumbs
> ¼ cup milk
> 4 egg yolks
> 4 egg whites
> ⅓ cup milk

Preheat oven to 350°. In large saucepan melt butter; add cheese. Cook and stir over low heat till cheese melts. Add *half* the soup, bread crumbs, and ¼ cup milk; stir till blended. Remove from heat. Beat egg yolks till thick and lemon-colored; gradually stir in hot mixture. Wash and dry beaters. Beat egg whites till stiff peaks form; fold in egg yolk mixture. Turn into *ungreased* 10x6x2-inch baking dish. Bake at 350° till knife inserted just off-center comes out clean, 25 to 30 minutes.

Meanwhile, for sauce stir together remaining soup and ⅓ cup milk. Heat through. Serve with soufflé. Serves 4 to 6.

Shrimp-Sauced Spaghetti

> 3 slices bacon
> ¼ cup chopped celery
> ¼ cup fresh or frozen chopped green
>   pepper
> 1 clove garlic, minced
> 1 15-ounce can tomato sauce with
>   onion
> ¾ cup water
> ¾ teaspoon dried basil, crushed
> ½ teaspoon dried oregano, crushed
> 1 4½-ounce can shrimp, drained
> 1 3-ounce can sliced mushrooms,
>   drained
> Hot cooked spaghetti

In saucepan cook bacon till crisp. Drain, reserving drippings, and crumble; set aside. Cook celery, green pepper, and garlic in reserved drippings till vegetables are tender but not brown. Stir in bacon, tomato sauce, water, basil, oregano, and ⅛ teaspoon pepper. Simmer, uncovered, till desired thickness, about 25 minutes. Stir in shrimp and mushrooms; heat through. Serve over spaghetti. Makes 4 servings.

Shrimp and Green Bean Bake

    1 4½-ounce can shrimp, drained
    1 9-ounce package frozen French-
        style green beans
    1 10½-ounce can condensed cream of
        celery soup
    2 tablespoons snipped parsley
    ¼ teaspoon grated lemon peel
    1 teaspoon lemon juice
    ½ cup shredded process American
        cheese (2 ounces)

Preheat oven to 350°. Rinse shrimp. Cook beans according to package directions *except* omit salt; drain. Place beans and shrimp in 1-quart casserole. Mix soup, parsley, peel, and juice; pour over shrimp mixture. Cover; bake at 350° for 15 minutes. Top with cheese; sprinkle with paprika, if desired. Bake, uncovered, till hot through, 5 to 10 minutes more. Serves 4.

Shrimp-Stuffed Fish

    1 3-pound fresh or frozen whitefish
        or other fish, boned and dressed
    ½ cup chopped celery
    ¼ cup fresh or frozen chopped green
        pepper
    ¼ cup fresh or frozen chopped onion
    6 tablespoons butter or margarine
    2 cups corn bread stuffing mix
    1 4½-ounce can shrimp, drained
    ¼ cup mayonnaise
    1 tablespoon snipped parsley
      Dash cayenne
    1 tablespoon cooking oil

Thaw frozen fish. Preheat oven to 350°. Pat fish dry with paper toweling; sprinkle inside generously with salt. Place in well-greased shallow baking pan. Cook celery, green pepper, and onion in butter till tender. Stir in stuffing mix and ⅓ cup water. Add shrimp, mayonnaise, parsley, and cayenne; mix well. Stuff fish loosely with mixture. (Bake extra stuffing in covered casserole for last 30 minutes.) Brush fish with oil. Cover; bake at 350° till fish flakes easily, 45 to 60 minutes. Serves 8.

Tuna-Rice Casserole

Preheat oven to 350°. In mixing bowl stir ⅓ cup milk into one 10½-ounce can condensed cream of shrimp soup. Add ¾ cup uncooked packaged precooked rice; one 3-ounce can sliced mushrooms, drained; 2 tablespoons mayonnaise or salad dressing; 2 tablespoons chopped canned pimiento; and 1 teaspoon instant minced onion. Fold in one 6½- or 7-ounce can tuna, drained and broken into pieces. Turn into a 1-quart casserole. Sprinkle with 2 tablespoons crumbled Cheddar cheese crackers. Cover; bake at 350° about 40 minutes. Serves 4.

Sole Caledonia

    1 pound fresh or frozen sole fillets
    ¾ cup dry white wine
    1 10-ounce package frozen cut
        asparagus, cooked and drained
    ½ cup halved cherry tomatoes
    ½ cup sliced fresh mushrooms
    2 tablespoons butter or margarine
    2 tablespoons all-purpose flour
    ½ teaspoon salt
      Dash white pepper
    1¼ cups milk
    1 slightly beaten egg yolk
    1 cup soft bread crumbs (1½ slices)
    ¼ cup grated Parmesan cheese

Thaw frozen fish. Preheat oven to 350°. In covered skillet cook sole fillets in ½ cup of the wine till fish flakes easily when tested with a fork, 2 to 3 minutes. Drain and arrange in 10x6x2-inch baking dish; season with a little salt. Top with asparagus, cherry tomatoes, and mushrooms. In small saucepan melt butter. Stir in flour, salt, and white pepper. Stir in milk; cook and stir till mixture thickens and bubbles. Stir a small amount of the hot mixture into the egg yolk; return to saucepan. Cook and stir till bubbly. Remove from heat; stir in the remaining wine. Pour evenly over fish and vegetables in baking dish. Combine the bread crumbs and Parmesan cheese. Sprinkle over top of fish. Bake, uncovered, at 350° for 30 minutes. Makes 4 servings.

Tuna Soufflé with Mushroom Sauce

1 teaspoon instant minced onion
1 cup milk
3 tablespoons butter or margarine
3 tablespoons all-purpose flour
¼ teaspoon paprika
1 6½- or 7-ounce can tuna, drained
    and flaked
1 tablespoon snipped parsley
4 egg yolks
4 stiffly beaten egg whites
    Mushroom Sauce

Preheat oven to 325°. Soften onion in milk. Melt butter; blend in flour, paprika, 1 teaspoon salt, and dash pepper. Add onion mixture. Cook and stir till thickened and bubbly. Remove from heat. Stir in tuna and parsley. Beat yolks till thick and lemon-colored. *Slowly* add tuna mixture, stirring constantly. Cool slightly. Add gradually to egg whites, folding together thoroughly. Turn into *ungreased* 5-cup soufflé dish. Bake at 325° till knife inserted off-center comes out clean, about 50 minutes. Serve at once with Mushroom Sauce. Serves 4.

Mushroom Sauce: Soften 1 teaspoon instant minced onion in 1 cup milk. In saucepan melt 2 tablespoons butter or margarine; blend in 2 tablespoons all-purpose flour, ¼ teaspoon salt, and dash pepper. Add milk mixture all at once. Cook and stir till thickened and bubbly. Stir in one 3-ounce can sliced mushrooms, drained, and 1 tablespoon dry sherry; heat through.

Salmon-Mac Pie

4 well-beaten eggs
2 15-ounce cans macaroni in cheese
    sauce
1 16-ounce can salmon, drained and
    broken into chunks
½ teaspoon salt

Preheat oven to 375°. Stir together eggs, macaroni and cheese, salmon, and salt. Turn into greased 10x6x2-inch baking dish. Bake at 375° till set, 30 to 35 minutes. Serve with catsup, if desired. Makes 4 servings.

Saucy Sausage Beefburgers

Good for a weekend brunch —

½ pound bulk pork sausage
½ pound ground beef
1½ cups soft bread crumbs (1½ slices
    bread)
3 tablespoons milk
½ teaspoon poultry seasoning
• • •
2 tablespoons all-purpose flour
¼ teaspoon paprika
1 10¾-ounce can condensed cream of
    mushroom soup
1 cup water
3 English muffins, split and toasted

In mixing bowl combine pork sausage, ground beef, bread crumbs, milk, and poultry seasoning. Shape into six patties. In skillet brown the patties; drain off excess fat. Stir flour and paprika into mushroom soup; gradually blend in water. Pour soup mixture around patties; cook over medium-low heat till meat is done, 15 to 20 minutes, stirring sauce occasionally. Serve one burger on each toasted muffin half. Spoon sauce over top of each sandwich. Serves 6.

Salami Stack-Ups

A good choice for supper —

8 slices rye bread
    Butter or margarine, softened
1 4-ounce container whipped cream
    cheese
• • •
8 slices salami (about 8 ounces)
¼ cup mustard-style hot dog relish
¼ cup chopped onion

Preheat oven to 400°. Spread one side of each slice bread with butter or margarine, then spread with whipped cream cheese. Place one slice salami atop *each of* 4 slices bread; spread with hot dog relish and sprinkle with chopped onion. Place remaining salami atop. Top with remaining bread. Wrap sandwiches individually in foil; bake at 400° till heated through, 25 to 30 minutes. Makes 4 sandwiches.

Bratwurst Sandwiches

Simmered in beer for a delightful flavor—

6 bratwurst links (12 ounces)
1 8-ounce can sauerkraut, drained
**   and snipped**
1 cup beer
2 teaspoons instant minced onion
1 teaspoon caraway seed
6 frankfurter buns, split and
**   toasted**

Place bratwurst links in large saucepan. Combine snipped sauerkraut, beer, instant minced onion, and caraway seed. Spoon mixture over sausage links. Cover; simmer for 30 minutes. Place bratwurst links in toasted frankfurter buns; spoon sauerkraut mixture over bratwurst links. Serves 6.

Hot Corned Beef Buns

2 cups finely shredded cabbage
1 12-ounce can corned beef, crumbled
½ cup mayonnaise or salad dressing
1 teaspoon instant minced onion
1 teaspoon horseradish mustard
8 hamburger buns, split and
**   buttered**
16 dill pickle slices

Preheat oven to 375°. Combine cabbage, corned beef, mayonnaise, minced onion, and horseradish mustard. Spread about ⅓ cup filling on bottom half of each hamburger bun; top each with two pickle slices and the other half of bun. Wrap individually in foil. Place on baking sheet. Bake at 375° till hot, about 20 minutes. Makes 8 servings.

Simmer up a potful of Hearty Chicken Soup *for supper after your day's work is done. No time to stew a chicken? Use canned chicken for meatiness, and add vegetables and herbs to give the soup distinctive flavor.*

Hearty Chicken Soup

Use either canned chicken or leftover cooked chicken to prepare this flavorful soup —

    3 cups water
    1 16-ounce can tomatoes, cut up
    1 carrot, sliced (½ cup)
    1 small onion, sliced (½ cup)
    ½ cup sliced celery
    1 teaspoon salt
    ¼ teaspoon dried thyme, crushed
    1 bay leaf
            •   •   •
    2 5-ounce cans boned chicken, cut
       up *or* 1½ cups diced cooked
       chicken
    1 cup uncooked medium noodles
    1 3-ounce can sliced mushrooms,
       drained

In large saucepan combine water, tomatoes, sliced carrot, onion, celery, salt, thyme, and bay leaf. Bring mixture to boiling; reduce heat. Simmer, covered, for 30 minutes. Remove bay leaf. Stir in diced chicken, uncooked noodles, and drained mushrooms. Boil gently, covered, till noodles are done, 8 to 10 minutes. Makes 5 or 6 servings.

Beef-Cabbage Soup

Serve buttered rye bread and dill pickle strips with this soup —

    2 cups coarsely chopped cabbage
    1 16-ounce can tomatoes, cut up
 1½ cups water
    1 tablespoon instant minced onion
    1 teaspoon instant beef bouillon
       granules
    1 teaspoon sugar
    ⅛ teaspoon pepper
    1 12-ounce can corned beef, broken
       into chunks

In large saucepan combine chopped cabbage, tomatoes, water, instant minced onion, beef bouillon granules, sugar, and pepper. Bring the mixture to boiling; reduce heat. Simmer, covered, till cabbage is tender, about 30 minutes. Stir in corned beef chunks; heat through. Serves 4 or 5.

Vegetable Chili

    1 pound ground beef
    1 cup fresh or frozen chopped onion
    1 16-ounce can tomatoes, cut up
    1 10-ounce package frozen mixed
       vegetables
    1 8-ounce can tomato sauce
    ¾ cup water
    1 to 2 teaspoons chili powder
    1 teaspoon salt

In saucepan cook beef and onion till beef is browned. Drain off fat. Stir in remaining ingredients. Cover; simmer till vegetables are done, about 40 minutes. Serves 4.

Beef-Corn Stew

    1 pound ground beef
    ½ cup fresh or frozen chopped onion
    3 large potatoes, peeled and diced
    1 17-ounce can cream-style corn
    1 10½-ounce can condensed beef
       broth

In large skillet brown beef and onion; drain off fat. Add remaining ingredients, 1 teaspoon salt, and dash pepper; mix well. Cover; cook over low heat for 20 to 25 minutes, stirring occasionally. Serves 4.

Easy Vegetable Soup

    2 13¾-ounce cans chicken broth
       (3½ cups)
    1 10-ounce package frozen mixed
       Italian *or* Spanish vegetables
    ⅓ cup catsup
    ¼ cup anellini (tiny hollow pasta
       circles) or macaroni
    2 tablespoons dried celery flakes
    1 tablespoon instant minced onion
    1 teaspoon Italian salad dressing
       mix

In large saucepan combine all ingredients. Bring to boiling; reduce heat. Cover and simmer till pasta is tender, about 30 minutes. Makes 5 or 6 servings.

Side Dishes and Desserts

Sangria Acapulco

½ orange
¼ cup sugar
1 ⅘-quart bottle dry red wine
⅔ cup orange-flavored liqueur
1 7-ounce bottle club soda
Cracked ice

Thinly slice outer peel from orange with vegetable peeler. Put peel in large pitcher with sugar. Bruise peel with back of spoon to release oils. Add wine and liqueur. Chill 15 minutes. Remove peel. Add soda. Garnish with thin orange slices, if desired. Serve in glasses with ice. Serves 6.

Deviled Nuts

1½ cups pecan halves (5 ounces)
1½ cups whole blanched almonds
    (8 ounces)
1 tablespoon butter, melted
1 tablespoon cooking oil
2 teaspoons celery salt
1½ teaspoons chili powder

Preheat oven to 300°. Place nuts in 13x9x2-inch baking pan. Mix remaining ingredients and 1 teaspoon salt. Drizzle over nuts; stir to coat. Bake at 300° till almonds are lightly browned, 25 to 30 minutes; stir often. Serve warm or cool. Makes 3 cups.

Creamy Lime Dressing

1 8-ounce carton plain yogurt
2 tablespoons honey
1 tablespoon syrup from canned
    fruit or milk
1 teaspoon grated lime peel

Combine all ingredients and dash salt; chill quickly in the freezer. Serve over fresh or canned fruit salad. Makes 1 cup dressing.

Fiesta Corn Bake

1 17-ounce can cream-style corn
1 8¼-ounce can sliced carrots,
    drained (1 cup)
¼ cup fresh or frozen chopped onion
¼ cup sliced pitted ripe olives
1 tablespoon snipped parsley
1¾ cups soft bread crumbs (3 slices)
2 beaten eggs
½ teaspoon salt
    Dash pepper
    Dash bottled hot pepper sauce
1 tablespoon butter or margarine,
    melted

Preheat oven to 350°. Combine corn, carrots, onion, olives, and parsley. Add 1 cup of the bread crumbs, eggs, salt, pepper, and hot pepper sauce. Pour into a 10x6x2-inch baking dish. Toss remaining crumbs with butter; sprinkle atop casserole. Bake at 350° for 40 minutes. Remove from oven; let stand 5 minutes before serving. Serves 6.

Ginger-Bean Bake

2 16-ounce cans pork and beans in
    tomato sauce
½ cup finely crushed gingersnaps
¼ cup catsup
2 tablespoons light molasses
½ teaspoon salt

Preheat oven to 350°. Combine all ingredients. Pour into 1-quart casserole. Bake, covered, at 350° till heated through, about 30 minutes. Makes 6 servings.

Special touches made easy

Side dishes and desserts that fit after work schedules → *include* Fiesta Corn Bake, Crab Apple-Peach Dumplings *(see recipe, page 92), and* Deviled Nuts.

Rice Pilaf

 1½ cups uncooked long grain rice
 ¼ cup fresh or frozen finely
     chopped onion
 3 tablespoons butter or margarine
 1 13¾-ounce can chicken broth

In 10-inch skillet cook rice and onion in butter until rice is golden, stirring often. Add broth, 1 cup water, and ½ teaspoon salt. Bring to boiling; reduce heat. Cover and simmer till tender, about 15 minutes. Fluff up with a fork. Makes 8 servings.

Hashed Brown Scallop

 1 16-ounce package frozen hashed
     brown potatoes, thawed (4 cups)
 1 cup shredded sharp process
     American cheese (4 ounces)
 ¼ cup sliced green onion
 1 chicken bouillon cube
 ½ cup boiling water
 1 tablespoon butter or margarine

Preheat oven to 375°. In 1½-quart casserole combine potatoes, cheese, and onion. Dissolve bouillon cube in boiling water; pour over potato mixture. Dot with butter. Cover; bake at 375° till potatoes are tender, about 30 minutes, stirring occasionally. If desired, top with triangles of sharp process American cheese. Bake till cheese melts, 1 to 2 minutes more. Makes 6 servings.

Peppy Potatoes

 1 2⅜-ounce package seasoned coating
     mix for chicken
 4 unpeeled potatoes, cut in 1-inch
     wedges
   Butter or margarine, melted

Preheat oven to 325°. Pour coating mix and ¼ teaspoon salt into a bag. Dip potatoes in melted butter, then shake, a few at a time, in coating mixture. Place on well-greased baking sheet. Bake at 325° till done, about 60 minutes. Makes 4 servings.

Apple-Filled Squash

 3 acorn squash
 5 tablespoons butter or margarine,
     melted
 1 18-ounce can pie-sliced apples
 ¾ cup packed brown sugar
 1 teaspoon lemon juice
 ¼ teaspoon ground ginger

Preheat oven to 350°. Halve squash lengthwise; remove seeds. Brush with *2 tablespoons* of the butter and sprinkle with salt. Place, cut side down, in large baking dish. Bake at 350° for 35 minutes. Combine apples, brown sugar, lemon juice, and ginger. Turn squash cut side up in baking dish. Fill centers with apple mixture. Drizzle with remaining butter. Continue baking till tender, about 25 minutes more. If desired, sprinkle with ground cinnamon. Serves 6.

Broccoli-Cheese Casserole

 2 10-ounce packages frozen chopped
     broccoli, cooked and drained
 1 11-ounce can condensed Cheddar
     cheese soup
 ¼ cup milk
 1 tablespoon butter or margarine
 ½ cup coarsely crumbled saltine
     crackers (12 crackers)

Preheat oven to 350°. Place broccoli in 1-quart casserole. Blend soup, milk, ¼ teaspoon salt, and dash pepper. Stir into broccoli. Melt butter; toss with crumbs. Sprinkle atop casserole. Bake at 350° till heated through, about 30 minutes. Serves 6.

Parslied Carrots

Preheat oven to 400°. Halve 8 medium carrots lengthwise. Place in a 10x6x2-inch baking dish. Stir in 2 tablespoons water, 2 tablespoons butter, 1 teaspoon sugar, ¼ teaspoon salt, and dash pepper. Cover tightly with foil; bake at 400° till tender, 45 to 50 minutes. Sprinkle with 2 teaspoons snipped parsley. Serves 4 to 6.

Six generous servings of Apple-Filled Squash are apple-pie easy to make when you add sugar and spice to canned pie-sliced fruit for the tasty filling.

Potato-Vegetable Scallop

A tasty way to dress up scalloped potatoes —

> 1 4⅝- or 5½-ounce package dry
>   scalloped potato mix
> 1 10-ounce package frozen mixed
>   vegetables
> ½ cup thinly sliced onion
> ¼ teaspoon celery seed
> 2½ cups boiling water
> 2 tablespoons butter or margarine
> ½ cup shredded sharp process
>   American cheese (2 ounces)

Preheat oven to 400°. Place dried potatoes from mix in 1½-quart casserole. Sprinkle with the envelope of sauce mix from package. Top with frozen mixed vegetables, sliced onion, and celery seed. Pour boiling water over all; stir till well combined. Dot with butter or margarine. Cover; bake at 400° till potatoes are tender, about 35 minutes. Uncover; sprinkle with shredded cheese. Return to oven till cheese melts, 2 to 3 minutes more. Makes 6 servings.

Cheesy Corn

A special way to fix corn on the cob —

> 6 ears fresh corn
>   • • •
> 1 4-ounce container whipped cream
>   cheese with chives
> ¼ cup butter or margarine, softened
> ¼ teaspoon salt
>   Dash pepper

Preheat oven to 400°. Remove husks from ears of corn; remove silk with stiff brush. In small bowl stir whipped cream cheese into butter; blend in salt and pepper. Place each ear of corn on a square of foil; spread each with a generous tablespoon of the cream cheese mixture. Fold up and seal foil. Bake at 400° till tender, about 45 minutes. Spoon hot cheese-butter mixture over corn to serve. Makes 6 servings.

Potato-Cheese Custard

Garnish with crumbled bacon —

> 2 cups diced potatoes
> 2 cups milk
> 1 5-ounce jar process cheese spread
>   with bacon
> 1 teaspoon instant minced onion
> 2 beaten eggs
> 1 tablespoon snipped parsley
> ½ teaspoon dry mustard
> ½ teaspoon salt
>   Dash pepper
>   Crumbled crisp-cooked bacon
>   (optional)

Preheat oven to 325°. In saucepan combine diced potatoes and enough water to cover; bring to boiling. Remove from heat; drain. Arrange cooked potatoes in 10x6x2-inch baking dish. Heat milk, cheese spread, and onion till cheese melts. Combine eggs, snipped parsley, dry mustard, salt, and pepper. Gradually stir hot milk mixture into eggs; pour over potatoes. Bake at 325° till knife inserted just off-center comes out clean, 35 to 40 minutes. Top with crumbled bacon, if desired. Let stand 5 minutes before serving. Makes 6 servings.

Cranberry Ring

Perfect for a weekend brunch—

½ cup cranberry-orange relish
1 tablespoon light corn syrup
• • •
½ cup packed brown sugar
¼ cup butter or margarine, melted
1 teaspoon ground cinnamon
2 packages refrigerated buttermilk
  biscuits (20 biscuits)

Preheat oven to 375°. In saucepan combine cranberry-orange relish and light corn syrup; heat just to boiling. Spoon mixture into greased 6½-cup ring mold. Combine brown sugar, melted butter or margarine, and cinnamon. Spread one side of each biscuit with some of the brown sugar mixture. Stand biscuits on edge in ring mold. Bake at 375° till done, about 25 minutes. Allow to cool in pan 3 minutes. Invert onto serving plate. Makes 20 rolls.

Protein-Plus Muffins

Serve these delicious muffins with a soup or salad to increase the protein in the meal—

1¼ cups soy flour
⅔ cup nonfat dry milk powder
2 teaspoons baking powder
½ teaspoon salt
½ cup chopped pitted dates
¼ cup chopped walnuts
• • •
2 slightly beaten eggs
1 teaspoon grated orange peel
¾ cup orange juice
2 tablespoons honey
2 tablespoons cooking oil

Preheat oven to 350°. In mixing bowl stir the soy flour, nonfat dry milk powder, baking powder, and salt together thoroughly. Stir in the chopped dates and chopped walnuts. Combine the beaten eggs, grated orange peel, orange juice, honey, and cooking oil. Stir the egg mixture into the dry ingredients just till moistened. Fill greased muffin cups ⅔ full. Bake at 350° till done, about 30 minutes. Makes 12 muffins.

Sour Cream-Chive French Loaves

2 loaves unsliced French bread
¾ cup butter or margarine, softened
½ cup dairy sour cream
2 tablespoons snipped chives
¼ teaspoon garlic powder

Preheat oven to 325°. Cut each loaf of bread lengthwise, then crosswise, *cutting to but not through* bottom crust. Mix remaining ingredients; spread on bread. Wrap in foil. Heat at 325° for 20 to 25 minutes. Serves 8.

Thyme-Buttered Crescents

½ cup butter or margarine, softened
1 teaspoon lemon juice
½ teaspoon dried thyme, crushed
1 package refrigerated crescent
  rolls (8 rolls)

Cream butter till fluffy. Stir in lemon juice and thyme. Keep herb butter at room temperature for 1 hour to mellow before using.

Preheat oven. Unroll crescents; spread *2 teaspoons* herb butter on each crescent. Roll crescents up and bake according to package directions. Serve hot. Makes 8 rolls.

Raspberry Coffee Cake

1 cup packed brown sugar
½ cup butter or margarine
1 egg
1 teaspoon vanilla
2 cups all-purpose flour
1 teaspoon baking soda
½ teaspoon baking powder
1 8-ounce carton raspberry yogurt

Preheat oven to 350°. Cream sugar and butter; add egg and vanilla. Stir flour, soda, baking powder, and ¼ teaspoon salt together; add alternately with yogurt to creamed mixture. Mix well. Pour into greased 9-inch tube pan. Bake at 350° for 50 minutes. Remove from pan; sprinkle with powdered sugar, if desired. Serve warm or cool. Makes 1 coffee cake.

Fruit Compote Supreme

Keep this flavorful baked compote in mind for cold weather menus —

    1 16-ounce can peach slices
    1 cup dried apricots
    ½ cup packed brown sugar
    1 teaspoon grated orange peel
    ⅓ cup orange juice
    ½ teaspoon grated lemon peel
    2 tablespoons lemon juice
           •   •   •
    1 16-ounce can pitted dark sweet
      cherries, drained

Preheat oven to 350°. In 10x6x2-inch baking dish combine undrained peach slices, dried apricots, brown sugar, grated orange peel, orange juice, grated lemon peel, and lemon juice. Cover and bake compote at 350° for 45 minutes. Gently stir in the dark sweet cherries. Bake, covered, till cherries are heated through, about 15 minutes longer. Makes 6 to 8 servings.

Peanut Butter-Banana Crunch

A dessert the whole family will enjoy —

    4 cups sliced bananas (6 medium
      bananas)
    1 tablespoon lemon juice
    ½ teaspoon ground cinnamon
           •   •   •
    ½ cup all-purpose flour
    ½ cup packed brown sugar
    ⅓ cup chunk-style peanut butter
    3 tablespoons butter or margarine
      Whipped cream or whipped dessert
      topping (optional)

Preheat oven to 375°. Place sliced bananas in 8x1½-inch round baking dish. Add lemon juice and ground cinnamon, stirring lightly to coat fruit. In small mixing bowl combine flour and brown sugar; cut in chunk-style peanut butter and butter or margarine till mixture is crumbly. Sprinkle peanut butter mixture over bananas. Bake at 375° for 25 minutes. Serve warm; top with dollops of whipped cream or whipped dessert topping, if desired. Makes 6 servings.

Coconut-Peach Upside-Down Cake

A cake mix makes this extra easy —

    ½ cup packed brown sugar
    ¼ cup flaked coconut
    3 tablespoons butter or margarine,
      melted
    1 8-ounce can peach slices, drained
    1 package 1-layer-size yellow cake
      mix

Preheat oven to 350°. In 8x1½-inch round baking dish combine brown sugar, coconut, and melted butter or margarine. Pat evenly in bottom of dish. Arrange peach slices over coconut mixture. Mix cake according to package directions. Spread carefully over peaches. Bake at 350° till done, about 40 minutes. Cool 2 minutes in dish; invert on plate to serve. Makes 6 servings.

Sour Cream-Rhubarb Squares

    ½ cup granulated sugar
    ½ cup chopped walnuts
    1 tablespoon butter or margarine,
      melted
    1 teaspoon ground cinnamon
           •   •   •
    1½ cups packed brown sugar
    ½ cup shortening
    1 egg
    2 cups all-purpose flour
    1 teaspoon baking soda
    ½ teaspoon salt
    1 cup dairy sour cream
    1½ cups rhubarb cut in ½-inch
       pieces

Preheat oven to 350°. In small bowl mix granulated sugar, chopped walnuts, melted butter or margarine, and ground cinnamon till crumbly; set aside. Cream together brown sugar, shortening, and egg. Stir flour, baking soda, and salt together thoroughly; add to creamed mixture alternately with dairy sour cream. Stir in rhubarb pieces. Turn into greased and floured 13x 9x2-inch baking pan. Sprinkle with crumbly mixture. Bake at 350° for 45 to 50 minutes. Serve warm. Makes 9 to 12 servings.

Ginger-Pear Dessert

Serve warm with ice cream —

    4 medium pears
    ¼ cup orange juice
    1 cup finely crushed gingersnaps
    ¼ cup sugar
    ¼ cup chopped walnuts
    ¼ cup butter or margarine, melted
        Vanilla ice cream

Preheat oven to 350°. Peel pears; halve and core. Place pear halves, cut side up, in 10x6x2-inch baking dish. Drizzle with orange juice. Combine finely crushed gingersnaps, sugar, walnuts, and melted butter or margarine; sprinkle over pear halves. Bake at 350° till pears are tender, 20 to 25 minutes. Serve warm; top with scoops of vanilla ice cream. Makes 8 servings.

Cherry Crumbles

    1 21-ounce can cherry pie filling
    1 package 1-layer-size yellow cake mix
    ¼ cup butter or margarine, melted

Preheat oven to 375°. Spread pie filling in buttered 8x8x2-inch baking pan; sprinkle with the dry cake mix. Drizzle with melted butter or margarine (*do not stir*). Bake at 375° till top is golden, 35 to 40 minutes. Serve warm. Makes 8 servings.

Crab Apple-Peach Dumplings

Frozen patty shells speed up the preparation of this dessert (shown on page 87)—

    6 frozen patty shells, thawed
    6 canned peach halves
    6 spiced crab apples, cored and halved
    1 3-ounce package cream cheese, cut in 6 sticks
        Maple-flavored syrup *or* frozen whipped dessert topping

Preheat oven to 400°. Roll out each patty shell to a 6-inch circle. Top *each* with a peach half, 2 apple halves, and a stick of cream cheese. Moisten edges of dough; fold to center, forming a triangle. Seal. Bake at 400° till golden brown, 20 to 25 minutes. Serve topped with maple syrup or frozen whipped topping. Makes 6 servings.

Banana-Coconut Betty

    2 cups soft bread crumbs (2½ slices bread)
    6 tablespoons butter or margarine, melted
    ⅓ cup sugar
    2 teaspoons grated orange peel
    ½ teaspoon ground nutmeg
    ½ teaspoon ground cinnamon
    4 cups sliced banana (4 or 5)
    ¼ cup orange juice
    ¼ cup water
    ½ cup flaked coconut

Preheat oven to 375°. Toss crumbs with melted butter or margarine to coat. Line a 1½-quart casserole with *one-third* of the crumb mixture. Combine sugar, orange peel, nutmeg, and cinnamon. Cover crumbs with *half* the sliced banana and *half* the sugar mixture. Cover with another *one-third* of the crumbs, the remaining banana, and remaining sugar mixture. Combine orange juice and water; spoon over. Toss the remaining crumbs with flaked coconut; sprinkle over all. Bake, covered, at 375° for 30 to 35 minutes. Uncover; bake till golden, 5 to 10 minutes more. Makes 6 servings.

Baked Coffee Custard

Test custards the easy way—insert a thin-bladed knife about ½ inch deep in the center going straight down. If the knife comes out clean, the custard is ready—

  2 eggs
  ⅓ cup sugar
  1½ teaspoons instant coffee crystals
  1½ cups milk, scalded
      Frozen whipped dessert topping, thawed
      Sliced almonds, toasted (optional)

Preheat oven to 325°. In a 4-cup measuring cup or bowl with a pouring lip, beat eggs slightly. Add sugar, coffee crystals, and dash salt; mix well. Gradually stir in scalded milk. On oven shelf place four 5-ounce custard cups in a shallow baking pan. Pour custard mixture into cups. Pour hot water around cups in pan to a depth of 1 inch. (Filling the pan and cups at the oven saves carrying the full pan across the room.) Bake custards at 325° till knife inserted in center comes out clean, 45 to 50 minutes. Remove custards from pan of hot water and serve warm or chilled. Garnish with dollops of whipped dessert topping and sprinkle with toasted almonds, if desired. Serves 4.

Apple-Coconut Dessert

  1 package 1-layer-size yellow cake mix
  1 3½-ounce can flaked coconut (1⅓ cups)
  ½ teaspoon ground cinnamon
  ¼ cup butter or margarine, melted
  1 21-ounce can apple pie filling
      Vanilla ice cream (optional)

Preheat oven to 350°. Combine dry cake mix, coconut, and cinnamon; stir in melted butter. Press *two-thirds* of the mixture into an ungreased 8x8x2-inch baking pan; spread with pie filling. Crumble remaining coconut mixture over filling. Bake at 350° for 55 minutes. Serve warm or cooled; spoon into dessert dishes. Top with scoops of vanilla ice cream, if desired. Serves 6.

Pumpkin-Rice Pudding

  1 16-ounce can pumpkin
  ¾ cup sugar
  1 teaspoon ground cinnamon
  ½ teaspoon salt
  ½ teaspoon ground ginger
  ¼ teaspoon ground cloves
  2 slightly beaten eggs
  1 13-ounce can evaporated milk (1⅔ cups)
  ⅔ cup uncooked packaged precooked rice
  ½ cup raisins
      Whipped cream, chopped nuts, or vanilla ice cream, softened

Preheat oven to 350°. Combine pumpkin, sugar, cinnamon, salt, ginger, and cloves; stir in eggs. Add evaporated milk, mixing well. Stir in rice and raisins. Place shallow baking pan on the oven shelf; set six 5-ounce custard cups in pan. Fill cups with pumpkin mixture; pour hot water around cups in pan to depth of 1 inch. Bake at 350° till knife inserted in center comes out clean, 25 to 30 minutes. Remove from pan of hot water; serve warm or chilled. Top with whipped cream, nuts, or ice cream. Serves 6.

Baked Apples in Wine

  4 large baking apples
  ¼ cup packed brown sugar
  ¼ teaspoon ground nutmeg
  4 teaspoons butter or margarine
  1 cup rosé wine
  ½ cup dairy sour cream (optional)
      Ground nutmeg (optional)

Preheat oven to 350°. Core apples; peel strip from top of each. Place apples in 8x 8x2-inch baking dish. Stir together brown sugar and ¼ teaspoon nutmeg; spoon into apple centers. Top each apple with 1 teaspoon of the butter; pour wine into baking dish. Bake, uncovered, at 350° till tender, about 1 hour; baste with wine occasionally. Serve warm. If desired, top each apple with a dollop of sour cream and sprinkle with additional nutmeg. Makes 4 servings.

Special Helps

Does meal planning stump you? Are you tired of carrying the same things in your lunch box day after day? Are you concerned about good nutrition but not sure how to make meals more nutritious?

On the following pages you'll find a wealth of important information that will help you. Use the meal planning ideas and the already-planned menus as guides for appetizing meals. Put new life in lunch box lunches with the simple suggestions given. And plan nutritious meals, using the Basic 4 as explained on page 99.

There are also hints to help you cook for one or two, a list of emergency substitutions, a glossary, and information on the staple groceries, basic equipment, and freezer storage.

Turn to this informative section frequently. It's here to help you.

Include this menu often in your meal plans. Your family will like the Ham-Potato Bake, Spicy Fruit Salad, *and* Mocha Toffee Parfaits. *(See the menu on page 102.)*

Meal Planning

Have you ever envied a friend's ability to come home from work and seemingly without trouble prepare and serve a delicious meal? If you think this ability is a talent reserved for just a few, you are mistaken. Anyone can serve appetizing, attractive meals. However, these meals don't just happen. You must plan them carefully.

As an after work cook, you'll find that the amount of time you have to prepare meals is one of the most important considerations in planning menus. However, your meals also must fit your budget and be nutritious, yet appeal to the family.

Set aside some time on the weekend or one evening a week to plan the meals for the week. Write down the menus and make a detailed shopping list at the same time. This way you can save time shopping with just one trip to the store and you can save time preparing because everything you need will be on hand.

Look through a variety of recipes and choose those that will fit your available time. After work meal preparation time is often short and usually can be utilized best by combining the three types of cooking pointed out in this book — make ahead, jiffy, and easy. For instance, serve a make-ahead main dish with a jiffy salad and an easy baked dessert. By stretching meal preparation out like this, you won't be rushed at the last minute. The menus on pages 100 to 103 are designed specifically for after work preparation, so use them often.

For good food buys, check the newspaper food ads. Take advantage of specials whenever you can. Use fresh fruits and vegetables when they are in season. All of these hints contribute to economical menus.

In the rush to get to work, breakfast frequently is missed. And lunch is often a sandwich and coffee. These habits make it particularly hard to fulfill your nutritional needs. To help make up for this, pay special attention to nutrition when planning meals (use the Basic 4, as explained on page 99, as a guide). Be sure that sometime during the day you get a good variety of dairy foods, vegetables and fruits, protein foods, and breads and cereals. The following steps will help you incorporate foods from the Basic 4 into your menus:

1. Select a main dish that will provide each family member with at least one serving from the Meat Group.

2. Add a complementary food from the Bread-Cereal Group.

3. Include a hot or cold vegetable.

4. Choose a fruit or vegetable salad that complements the main dish.

5. Top off the meal with a dessert. Remember, fresh fruit makes a simple, yet nutritious dessert.

6. Select a hot or cold beverage. This is an excellent place to fulfill the daily milk requirement. If your family balks at drinking milk, disguise it by using it frequently in desserts such as puddings, custards, and even malts.

But using the Basic 4 won't do any good if the food is unpalatable. Delicious meals depend on a complementary blend of flavors and textures. The following tips will help you plan the right blend of foods:

● Serve a crisp food with a soft food.

● Accent a bland flavor with a zippy or tart food. Imagine the flavor of each food to determine which accent will blend.

● Season carefully to accent, not overwhelm, the flavor of the food. Usually, one highly seasoned food per meal is enough.

● Serve only one starchy food at each meal — potatoes, rice, macaroni, spaghetti, noodles, and sometimes squash or corn. The exception is bread or rolls, which you can serve with almost any meal.

● Plan a dessert that fits with the meal — a light dessert with a hearty meal, a rich dessert with a light meal.

● Accent hot foods with a cold food accompaniment. Temperature is important — serve hot foods hot and cold foods cold.

● Limit the number of mixtures served in a meal. For example, when serving a casserole, complement it with a gelatin square or lettuce wedge rather than with a tossed vegetable or mixed fruit salad.

Although your family is bound to have a few favorite dishes, don't get into a rut and serve only these favorites. Add variety to meals by trying a new food, a new seasoning, or a new way of preparing an old favorite. However, try only one new food per meal, especially with young children.

Look also to eye appeal. Serving an attractive meal contributes greatly to your family's and guests' enjoyment of the meal. The color of the food is one of the most important factors in making a meal attractive. Choose a variety of colors, yet make sure that the colors are complementary. If the food has little color, add a colorful vegetable or salad, or accent the food with a bright garnish such as parsley, cherry tomatoes, or paprika. Also, make sure that the color of the plates and serving dishes doesn't overwhelm the food.

A variety of shapes is also an important factor for an appetizing meal. Fruits and vegetables, especially, can be served in many shapes including whole, slices, wedges, cubes, and mashed.

A pleasing table setting greatly enhances the food's appearance, too. Although your meal preparation time is limited, take a few minutes before each meal to cover the table with a clean, colorful tablecloth, set plates and silverware neatly, and perhaps even add a pretty rose or other fresh or dried flowers as a centerpiece. This will make family as well as company meals more enjoyable.

Meal planning isn't difficult if you remember the hints on these pages. And as with any job well done, the satisfaction and the compliments of your family and guests will amply reward your efforts.

Lunch–Take It with You

In these days of hurried lunch hours and crowded lunch counters, carrying a lunch to work often is advantageous. However, packing an attractive and delicious lunch box lunch tests your ingenuity. Use the following appealing lunch box ideas to help you meet this challenge:

• Sandwiches are by far the most frequent lunch box food. Conserve time by making a week's supply of sandwiches at once and storing them in the freezer. (See box on page 21 for sandwich fillings that freeze well.) Transfer the sandwiches right from the freezer to the lunch box, and they will be just right for lunch.

• Keep the noon-hour sandwiches exciting by alternating breads on different days. Use white, rye, whole wheat, and nut breads, and perk up your sandwiches with lettuce and tomato slices. To ensure freshness, wrap these vegetables separately in foil or clear plastic wrap, then add them to the sandwich at lunchtime.

• Besides sandwiches, there are a host of other foods you can take along in your lunch box. Take advantage of the wide-mouth vacuum containers, which keep cold foods cold and hot foods hot, by packing chilled desserts, custard, pudding, tossed salads, gelatin salads, or canned fruits, as well as hot soup, stews, or casseroles. The handy wide mouth makes it easy to spoon the food out of the container. Small plastic containers with airtight seals also are great for lunch boxes because they help prevent spilled food.

• If even your spare time is too limited for lunch box preparation, buy ready-to-travel foods, such as cakes, breads, cheeses, potato chips, pickles, crackers, and even canned puddings, in serving-size containers. Pack a small can of frozen vegetable or fruit juice as a meal starter or beverage. It will be thawed but still cold at lunchtime. Fresh fruit wrapped in clear plastic wrap is an easy dessert to pack. Or, take along a frosted cupcake. To protect the frosting, invert a paper cup over the cupcake.

Although packing lunches sometimes seems tedious, you'll find lunchtime is more enjoyable if you take the time to add a few extras to your lunch box.

Think Good Nutrition

Does the phrase "eat a balanced diet" conjure up unpleasant memories of classroom lectures and scoldings from Mom and Dad? If so, it's time to revise your thinking and realize that practicing good nutrition is vital to your health. And that nutritious food is delicious.

It's easy to fall into poor nutritional habits. Perhaps you are too rushed to eat a good meal. Then, combine the four food groups into one dish such as a meat, tomato, and cheese sandwich or a macaroni, meat, tomato, and cheese skillet dish.

Or, maybe you don't like milk. If that's true, disguise milk by using it in cream sauces for meats or vegetables and in desserts such as custards and puddings.

Or, perhaps you live alone and it's too much bother to prepare a full meal, so you live on snacks. First, to take care of cooking in small quantities, follow the hints on page 91 and use the recipes for two servings given throughout the book. Then, use snacks as a nutritional supplement to meals. Eat fresh fruit instead of candy, a milk shake instead of pop, or a peanut butter sandwich instead of cookies.

Or, you might not be able to afford meat. Cut down meat costs by serving smaller portions (3 ounces lean cooked meat is an adequate portion); by making the meat go farther in casseroles, soups, stews, and main dish salads; and by planning some meals around protein foods other than meat.

As you can see, the reasons for poor nutrition could go on and on. However, by changing your ideas slightly, you can eliminate these stumbling blocks. In short, learn the Basic 4 (given at the right) and then *think good nutrition* at mealtime or whenever you eat.

Basic four ingenuity

← *For good health and good eating, plan daily meals that include the Dairy Group, the Meat Group, the Vegetable-Fruit Group, and the Bread-Cereal Group.*

Dairy Group: Milk is the primary source of calcium, which is needed for strong teeth and bones. It also provides protein, riboflavin, phosphorus, and vitamins A and D. Adults should drink *at least 2 cups daily;* teen-agers, 4 cups; children over nine, 3 cups; and children under nine, 2 to 3 cups. Cheese and ice cream may replace part of the daily requirement of milk. A 1-inch cube of Cheddar cheese=$\frac{2}{3}$ cup milk; $\frac{1}{2}$ cup cottage cheese=$\frac{1}{3}$ cup milk; 2 tablespoons cream cheese=1 tablespoon milk; and $\frac{1}{2}$ cup ice cream=$\frac{1}{4}$ cup milk.

Vegetable-Fruit Group: Include *4 or more servings* from this group daily to provide vitamins C and A and other nutrients. Every day choose one top source of vitamin C (grapefruit, oranges, cantaloupe, broccoli, peppers, or strawberries) or two fair sources (cabbage, potatoes, spinach, tangerines, or tomatoes). Every other day serve a good source of vitamin A (apricots, broccoli, cantaloupe, carrots, dark green leaves, spinach, sweet potatoes, or winter squash).

Meat Group: These are the protein foods needed for growth and repair of body tissues. They also provide iron, thiamine, niacin, riboflavin, and other nutrients. You need *2 servings a day* from this group. One serving is 2 to 3 ounces of poultry, fish, or lean cooked meat; 2 eggs; 1 cup cooked dried beans, peas, or lentils; $\frac{1}{4}$ cup peanut butter; or 2 ounces Cheddar, American, or Swiss cheese.

Bread-Cereal Group: Whole grain, enriched, or restored breads and cereals are rich sources of thiamine, niacin, riboflavin, and other nutrients. Check package labels to be sure your choice has been enriched. Choose *4 or more servings daily* from breads, cereals, cornmeal, crackers, flour, grits, macaroni, spaghetti, noodles, rice, quick breads, or other baked products. Count 1 slice of bread, 1 ounce of ready-to-eat cereal, or $\frac{1}{2}$ cup cooked cereal, rice, macaroni, or grits as one serving.

Menus

When preparing a meal, you may want to combine recipes for dishes that are prepared ahead, quickly, or leisurely. The following menus include recipes from all sections of this book. These various menus will enable you to fit your own after work time schedule.

Main Dish	Accompaniments	Salad	Dessert	Preparation Hints
Cauliflower-Tuna Ahoy (see page 8)	buttered French bread spiced peaches	lettuce wedge with Chili Mayonnaise (see page 58)	Mocha Toffee Parfaits (see page 64)	Prepare dressing and parfaits while main dish bakes. Serves 4.
Marinated Beef Tenderloin (see page 11)	Horseradish Bloody Mary (see page 26) Parker House rolls butter	Lemon-Blueberry Salad (see page 30)	Grasshopper Pie (see page 34)	Make-ahead menu for entertaining 6 guests. Serve the drink as an appetizer.
Apricot-Sauced Pork Chops (see page 10)	baked potatoes hard rolls butter	shredded cabbage with Herb Mayonnaise (see page 58)	Strawberry-Cheese Topping (see page 65) angel cake	Heat pork chops and bake the potatoes together in oven. Menu makes 6 servings.
Orange Chicken (see page 17)	Creamy Skillet Potatoes (see page 60) buttered broccoli	radishes carrot sticks	brownies	Prepare chicken main dish ahead. Serves 3 or 4.
Oriental Skillet (see page 13)	chow mein noodles Thyme-Buttered Crescents (see page 90)	Spicy Fruit Salad (see page 29)	tapioca pudding	Make basic beef mixture for main dish ahead. Serves 4.
Sausage Lasagne (see page 19)	Toasted Bun Sticks (see page 61)	lettuce wedge Italian dressing	Creamy Apricot Dessert (see page 35)	Assemble lasagne casserole ahead, then bake with bun sticks. Makes 6 servings.
Sweet-Sour Chicken Mold (see page 22)	Horseradish Bloody Mary (see page 26) hot rolls		Blueberry-Orange Nut Bread (see page 32) whipped butter	Ideal luncheon menu. Make recipes ahead; serve drink as appetizer. Serves 8.
Dill-Sauced Salmon (see page 8)	Zucchini with Walnuts (see page 60) whole wheat rolls butter	orange and grapefruit sections Italian dressing	Strawberry-Peach Sundae (see page 64) vanilla ice cream	Extra special dinner for entertaining. Flame sundaes at the table. Serves 4.

Main Dish	Accompaniments	Salad	Dessert	Preparation Hints
Chicken Roll-Ups (see page 16)	Parslied Carrots (see page 88) hard rolls	molded fruit salad	lemon sherbet sugar cookies	Bake chicken and carrots together. Menu serves 4.
Barbecue-Sauced Kabobs (see page 41)	parslied rice cherry tomatoes celery	Frosty Fruit Salad (see page 28)	angel cake	Prepare salad ahead. Serve kabobs with extra sauce. Serves 4.
Cheesy Tuna (see page 42)	baked patty shells	Tomato-Cucumber Marinade (see page 26)	Pumpkin-Rice Pudding (see page 93)	An impressive, yet easy-to-prepare dinner menu for 6.
Ham Barbecue (see page 45)	hot cooked rice Deviled Green Beans (see page 60)	fruit salad with Creamy Lime Dressing (see page 86)	Coffee-Banana Smoothee (see page 65)	The creamy-smooth dessert is made in a blender. Serves 2.
Saucy Poached Fish (see page 43)	hot cooked rice Pea Pods with Mushrooms (see page 60)	spiced apple rings	Baked Coffee Custard (see page 93)	Dessert bakes while rest of meal cooks on range. Serves 4.
Beef-Tomato Skillet (see page 38)	hot cooked noodles	pear halves with Pink Fruit Dressing (see page 58)	chocolate pudding frozen whipped dessert topping	Cook main dish for 4 atop the range. Meal is ready to dish up in less than ½ hour.
Apricot-Glazed Ham (see page 45)	Hashed Brown Scallop (see page 88) hard rolls	fresh or canned fruit cup with Citrus Dressing (see page 26)	Banana-Coconut Betty (see page 92)	Make dressing ahead. Potatoes and dessert bake at the same temperature. Serves 6.
Oriental Chicken (see page 47)	chow mein noodles *or* hot cooked rice	tossed salad with Herb Mayonnaise (see page 58)	Chocolate Layer Pie (see page 34)	Fix pie ahead. Begin with a white dinner wine. Serves 4 to 6.
Sausage and Hashed Brown Omelet (see page 48)	rusks butter	spiced crab apples	Polynesian Parfaits (see page 35)	An ideal supper menu. Makes 4 servings.
Cauliflower-Ham Chowder (see page 54)	rye rolls butter	Curried Pear and Cheese Salad (see page 56)	Apple-Coconut Dessert (see page 93) ice cream	Dessert bakes while you prepare chowder and salad. Serves 6.
Chicken-Wild Rice Skillet (see page 71)	hot rolls	cantaloupe wedge with green grapes	Pink Cream Dessert (see page 65)	Quick and easy menu for last-minute company. Serves 4.

Main Dish	Accompaniments	Salad	Dessert	Preparation Hints
Apple-Raisin Topped Ham (see page 72)	buttered corn Protein-Plus Muffins (see page 90)	Cottage Cheese-Cucumber Salad (see page 30)	pound cake	Ham and muffins bake together; make salad ahead. Serves 6.
Applesauce-Pork Loaf (see page 73)	Quick Glazed Sweet Potatoes (see page 60) spiced crab apples	lettuce wedge with green goddess dressing	ice cream cookies	Unusual applesauce-topped loaf will soon become a family favorite. Serves 4.
Lemony Lamb Chops (see page 78)	apple and orange slices mashed potatoes	Lima Salad (see page 58)	Fruit Compote Supreme (see page 91)	Chops and dessert bake together while you make the salad. Menu serves 6.
Swiss and Frank Pie (see page 79)	buttered carrots	sliced tomatoes and cucumbers with Herb Mayonnaise (see page 58)	Speedy Strawberry Parfaits (see page 65) ladyfingers	This main dish is nearly a complete meal in itself. Makes 6 servings.
Shrimp-Sauced Spaghetti (see page 81)	hot cooked spaghetti French bread with garlic butter buttered peas	orange slices and pineapple rings Italian dressing	Baked Coffee Custard (see page 93)	An unusual, easy-to-prepare spaghetti sauce. Menu serves 4.
Vegetable Chili (see page 85)	Thyme-Buttered Crescents (see page 90) carrot sticks cheese sticks	molded fruit salad	vanilla pudding	An extra-easy chili that uses frozen mixed vegetables. Makes 4 servings.
Ham-Potato Bake (see page 72) *(shown on page 94)*	relishes	Spicy Fruit Salad (see page 29)	Mocha Toffee Parfaits (see page 64)	Make salad ahead. While casserole bakes, make the parfaits. Serves 4 generously.
Oriental Stuffed Steaks (see page 77)	hard rolls asparagus spears with hollandaise sauce	tossed salad with blue cheese dressing	Butter-Rum Sundae (see page 65) vanilla ice cream	An elegant menu for entertaining. Accompany with rosé. Menu makes 6 servings.
Polynesian Pork Steaks (see page 73)	mashed potatoes relishes	sliced tomatoes with French dressing	Crab Apple-Peach Dumplings (see page 92) maple syrup *or* frozen whipped topping	A good menu for a special family occasion for 6. Meat simmers while you fix the rest of the meal.

Main Dish	Accompaniments	Salad	Dessert	Preparation Hints
Stroganoff Steak Sandwiches (see page 21)	Festive Cheese Ball (see page 26)	Spicy Fruit Salad (see page 29)	Chocolate-Marsh-mallow Pie (see page 33)	Guests enjoy the appetizer while you take a little time to finish the sand-wiches. Serves 6.
Ham Loaf Sandwiches (see page 20)	radishes celery	Italian Macaroni Salad (see page 28)	Cranberry-Apple-sauce-Oat Cake (see page 32)	A tasty picnic menu. Pack the sandwiches and salad in an ice chest. Serves 6.
Potato-Topped Stew (see page 14)	Parsley-Onion Bread (see page 61)	sliced tomatoes	canned peaches	Make the stew ahead and freeze. Then, prepare the rest of the meal while stew bakes. Serves 4.
Meatball Hot Pot (see page 38)	Stir-Fried Green Beans (see page 59) hard rolls	Frosty Fruit Salad (see page 28)	angel cake	Guests participate in cooking the fondue-style main dish. Serves 4.
Broiled Meat Loaf (see page 40)	Sour Cream Potatoes (see page 61) carrots		Coffee-Banana Smoothee (see page 65)	A speedy meal for 2. Make the dessert in the blender.
Chicken Dinner Omelet (see page 48)	Deviled Green Beans (see page 60)	lettuce wedge with Italian salad dressing	pound cake topped with strawberries	Delight a drop-in guest with this menu for 2 made with ingredients you can keep on hand.
Speedy Chicken Chasseur (see page 46)	buttered rice buttered peas	spiced peaches carrots	Polynesian Parfaits (see page 35)	The main dish is a fix-up for carry-out chicken. Serves 4.
Chicken Pilaf (see page 68)	Deviled Green Beans (see page 60)	orange slices with Pink Fruit Dress-ing (see page 58)	butterscotch pudding	Fix the vegetable and salad quickly, then relax while the main dish bakes. Menu serves 2.
Hearty Chicken Soup (see page 85)	Cheesy Biscuits (see page 62)		Creamy Apricot Dessert (see page 35)	A perfect supper for a winter evening. Serves 6.

Food Storage Guide

Proper storage of food will save the food's good flavor and your money. So, promptly unpack groceries and store as directed:
Fresh Vegetables: Store white potatoes, sweet potatoes, onions, and winter squash unwashed in a cool, dry, dark place with good ventilation. Wash and thoroughly drain salad greens, celery, green onions, asparagus, and cabbage. Refrigerate separately in moisture-vaporproof bags. Remove tops of carrots, beets, and radishes; refrigerate separately in moisture-vaporproof bags. Husked sweet corn may be refrigerated in moisture-vaporproof bag for a short period of time. Leave peas in the pod and refrigerate.
Fresh Fruit: Remove injured fruit before storing. Refrigerate ripe tomatoes, apples, oranges, lemons, grapefruit, limes, kumquats, tangerines, peaches, apricots, cherries, grapes, pears, plums, and rhubarb in a loosely covered container or perforated moisture-vaporproof bag to reduce drying or wilting. Store bananas, melons, avocados, and pineapple at cool room temperature. Store berries in the refrigerator; wash before serving.

To ripen fruit, place in well-ventilated area at room temperature; avoid direct sunlight. Tomatoes, peaches, bananas, avocados, pears, and plums can be ripened this way. Refrigerate the ripened fruit, except bananas, till ready to use.
Dried Fruit, Nuts: Store dried fruit in tightly closed container at room temperature. Nuts will keep longer if refrigerated in tightly covered containers.
Canned Foods: Store in cool, dry place. After a canned food has been opened, cover the can and store in refrigerator.
Flour, Cereals: Store at room temperature in tight containers.
Dairy Products: Tightly cover cottage cheese, hard and soft cheeses, milk, and butter and store in the refrigerator. Place strong-flavored cheeses in a tightly covered jar and store in the refrigerator.
Eggs: Refrigerate in a covered container or in the original carton. You can keep egg yolks for 2 to 3 days by refrigerating in tightly covered container. Egg whites will keep for a week to 10 days if refrigerated in a tightly covered container.
Meat, Poultry, Fish: Fresh meat, paper-wrapped from the butcher, should be rewrapped loosely in waxed paper before refrigerating. You can refrigerate fresh meat prepackaged in moisture-vaporproof wrap as is. If meat is to be frozen, wrap in moisture-vaporproof freezer wrap to prevent drying out of the surface. (Prepackaged meat can be frozen for 1 to 2 weeks without rewrapping. For longer storage, open the package and rewrap in moisture-vaporproof freezer wrap.) Refrigerate cured meat and luncheon meat in original wrap. Most canned hams need refrigeration (see label instructions). Refrigerate fish in moisture-vaporproof bags or tightly covered containers. Cool and refrigerate cooked meat promptly; when chilled, cover the meat to prevent drying.

For maximum quality, store meat, poultry, or fish in the refrigerator or freezer only for the length of time recommended in the chart below.

Maximum Storage Time		
Meat or Poultry	Refrigerator (36°-40° F)	Freezer (0° F or lower)
Beef	2 to 4 days	6 to 12 months
Pork	2 to 4 days	3 to 6 months
Ground meats	1 to 2 days	3 months
Frankfurters	4 to 5 days	1 month
Bacon	5 to 7 days	1 month
Ham	1 week	2 months
Ham slices	3 to 4 days	2 months
Variety meats	1 to 2 days	3 months
Luncheon meats	1 week	don't freeze
Bulk pork sausage	1 week	2 months
Smoked sausage	3 to 7 days	don't freeze
Dry sausage	2 to 3 weeks	don't freeze
Cooked meats	4 to 5 days	2 to 3 months
Chicken	1 to 2 days	12 months
Turkey	1 to 2 days	6 months
Fish	1 to 2 days	6 to 9 months

Cooking for One or Two

Cooking in small quantities often poses a problem because most recipes serve four or more. This generally means that you cook a large meal and then eat leftovers for days or else you fix hamburgers and frozen dinners time after time. You can be more creative than this. Use the following suggestions and the recipes for two from this book (see list at beginning of index):

• If you have freezer space, freeze meats and leftover main dishes in meal-size portions. Leftovers will seem like new if you haven't had the dish for a while. Shape ground beef into patties before freezing. Wrap the beef patties individually in waxed paper or clear plastic wrap so you can use them one at a time.

• Buy frozen vegetables in plastic bags. Then, remove and cook just what's needed.

• Keep frozen fish on hand for quick meals. Cut the package of fish in half while frozen and return half to the freezer. Poach the fish in salted water and serve with hollandaise sauce made from a mix.

• Eggs and cheese are great for small-size entrées. For example, try omelets filled with leftover vegetables and bits of cooked meat, poached eggs topped with a cheese sauce, or grilled cheese sandwiches topped with a slice of tomato or onion.

• Add variety to meats with sauces and gravies made from mixes.

• Fill out meals with delicatessen foods.

• Create a main dish salad from lettuce, raw or cooked vegetables, cheese strips, croutons, strips of luncheon meat or leftover meat, and/or hard-cooked egg. Serve with your favorite salad dressing.

Recipe Terms to Know

Baste – To moisten foods during cooking with pan drippings or a flavorful sauce.

Beat – To make mixture smooth by briskly whipping or stirring with a spoon, rotary beater, or electric mixer.

Blend – To thoroughly mix two or more ingredients until smooth and uniform.

Chop – To cut in small pieces.

Cream – To beat with a spoon or electric mixer till smooth, light, and fluffy.

Cut in – To mix shortening with dry ingredients using pastry blender or knives.

Dice – To cut food into small cubes of uniform size and shape.

Flake – To break lightly into small pieces.

Fold – To add ingredients gently to a mixture. Using a spatula, cut down through mixture; go across bottom of bowl and up and over, close to surface. Turn bowl frequently for even distribution.

Grate – To rub on a grater that separates the food into very fine particles.

Knead – To work the dough with the heel of the hand with a pressing, folding motion.

Marinate – To allow a food to stand in a seasoned liquid.

Mince – To cut or finely chop food into very small pieces.

Partially set – To chill gelatin until the consistency of egg white.

Poach – To simmer in liquid, being careful that food holds its shape while cooking.

Roast – To cook uncovered without liquid added, usually in an oven.

Shred – To rub on a shredder to form long, narrow pieces.

Simmer – To cook in liquid over low heat so that bubbles form at a slow rate and burst before reaching the surface.

Soft peaks – To beat egg whites or whipping cream till peaks are formed when beaters are lifted, but tips curl over.

Stiff peaks – To beat egg whites till peaks stand up straight when beaters are lifted, but are still moist and glossy.

Whip – To beat rapidly to incorporate air and produce expansion, as in whipping cream or egg whites.

Emergency Substitutions

For best recipe results, use the ingredients the recipe calls for. However, if you must substitute, consult the list in this chart.

In Place Of	Substitute
1 clove garlic	⅛ teaspoon garlic powder or instant minced garlic
1 small onion	1 teaspoon onion powder or 1 tablespoon instant minced onion, rehydrated
1 tablespoon fresh snipped herbs	1 teaspoon dried herbs
1 cup whipping cream, whipped	2 cups whipped dessert topping
1 cup cake flour	1 cup minus 2 tablespoons all-purpose flour
1 tablespoon cornstarch (for thickening)	2 tablespoons all-purpose flour or 4 teaspoons quick-cooking tapioca
1 cup sour milk or buttermilk	1 tablespoon lemon juice or vinegar plus whole milk to make 1 cup (let mixture stand 5 minutes before using)
1 1-ounce square unsweetened chocolate	3 tablespoons unsweetened cocoa powder plus 1 tablespoon butter or margarine
1 teaspoon dry mustard	1 tablespoon prepared mustard
1 cup tomato juice	½ cup tomato sauce plus ½ cup water
1 cup honey	1¼ cups sugar plus ¼ cup liquid
1 teaspoon baking powder	¼ teaspoon baking soda plus ½ cup buttermilk or sour milk (to replace ½ cup of liquid called for in recipe)
1 cup whole milk	½ cup evaporated milk plus ½ cup water or 1 cup reconstituted nonfat dry milk plus 2½ teaspoons butter or margarine
1 whole egg	2 egg yolks (for use in custards)
1 cup catsup or chili sauce	1 cup tomato sauce plus ½ cup sugar and 2 tablespoons vinegar (for use in cooked mixtures)
1 cake compressed yeast	1 package or 2 teaspoons active dry yeast

Stocking Your Kitchen

The after work cook (in fact, any cook) who has never stocked a kitchen before often has many problems. How many pots and pans should you buy? Which items from the variety of equipment do you really need? How do you know what is the best buy? What basic groceries must you have? The following guidelines will help you decide how to fill your kitchen with essentials:

• Purchase the best quality that you can afford. Remember, however, that high prices don't always mean good quality. Before buying a product, compare the material, design, special features, service contract, and warranty for different brands. Also read any available research studies.

• Pick out pieces that you can use for more than one job, such as freezer-to-oven-to-table baking dishes and casseroles and oven-going skillets.

• Every saucepan and skillet needs a securely fitting cover. Make sure that cover knobs and handles are made of a non-heat-conducting material.

• Avoid buying items with hard-to-clean cracks or unnecessary sharp edges.

• Make sure that each item is durable, stainproof, and rustproof.

• Look for seals of approval, standards, and testing. (Gas appliances should have the American Gas Association seal. Look for the Underwriters' Laboratory seal on all electrical equipment.)

• Read the warranty and make sure that servicing is readily available.

Basic kitchen equipment: The equipment needed for food preparation can be broken down into five groups—preparation, storage, cooking, cleaning, and serving. The variety of equipment available can be overwhelming, but remember that it isn't necessary to have everything. The following list is the equipment needed initially to supply a kitchen. Purchase other less essential equipment when necessary.

Preparation: Can opener, carving knife, slicer, grater or shredder, vegetable peeler, potato masher, kitchen shears, vegetable brush, pair of tongs, strainers, two paring knives, colander, serrated knife, electric mixer, nested set of dry measuring cups, wooden spoons, flour sifter, measuring spoons, rotary beater, set of mixing bowls, bottle opener, liquid measuring cup, rubber spatulas, rolling pin with cover, and pastry cloth.

Storage: Refrigerator/freezer, assorted refrigerator-freezer dishes, cupboards, foil, clear plastic wrap, bread box, canisters, and waxed paper.

Cooking: Covered skillets (10- and 7- to 8-inch), covered saucepans (1-, 2-, and 4- to 6-quart), range with oven, square baking pans, wire cooling rack, coffee maker, pancake turner, long-handled fork, toaster, long-handled spoon, oblong baking pan (13x9x2), round baking pans, loaf baking dish (8½x4½x2½), roasting pan with rack, muffin pan, custard cups, casserole with cover, cookie sheets, potholders, hot pads, and pie plates.

Cleaning: Sink, dishpan, dishcloth and towels, wastebasket, draining rack and mat, garbage pail, and wastepaper basket.

Serving: Serving bowls, dinner and salad plates, platter, sauce dishes, cups, saucers, glasses, table linen, and silverware.

Basic groceries: Most foods you buy are a matter of preference, but there are some things you can't cook without. Buy these things in quantities that you can use up within a reasonable amount of time. When buying perishable foods, choose the form—fresh, canned, dried, or frozen—that best fits your needs and storage facilities. When you start to run low on an item, jot it down for your next shopping trip.

Always keep these foods on hand: Sugar, all-purpose flour, salt, pepper, baking powder, baking soda, coffee and/or tea, shortening, salad oil, butter and/or margarine, your favorite herbs and spices, vanilla, mayonnaise and/or salad dressing, prepared mustard, Worcestershire sauce, catsup, bread, eggs, meat, salad greens, vegetables, fruits, juices, and milk.

INDEX